Dispute and Conflict Resolution in Plymouth County, Massachusetts, 1725–1825

Studies in Legal History

Published by The University of North Carolina Press
in association with the
American Society for Legal History

Dispute and Conflict Resolution in Plymouth County, Massachusetts, 1725–1825

by WILLIAM E. NELSON

The University of North Carolina Press
Chapel Hill

To LEILA

Manufactured in the United States of America

Library of Congress Cataloging in Publication Data

Nelson, William Edward, 1940–
Dispute and conflict resolution in Plymouth County, Massachusetts, 1725–1825.

(Studies in legal history)
Bibliography: p.
Includes index.
1. Justice, Administration of—Massachusetts—Plymouth Co.—History. 2. Courts—Massachusetts—Plymouth Co.—History. 3. Plymouth Co., Mass.—History. I. Title. II. Series.
KFM2999.P6N44 347'744'82 80-17403
ISBN 0-8078-1454-7

Contents

Tables

Acknowledgments

In two significant respects, this book grows out of my earlier research in the legal history of Massachusetts, which was published under the title *Americanization of the Common Law: The Impact of Legal Change on Massachusetts Society, 1760–1830*.

First, the results of that earlier research have framed the issues which this study addresses. *Americanization* attempted to construct a coherent portrait of late eighteenth- and early nineteenth-century legal doctrine on the basis of that part of the law which could be analyzed in greatest detail: the rules of civil procedure. The book's central finding, on which the remainder of its analysis rested, was that eighteenth-century juries possessed power to determine law as well as fact. That finding, in turn, raised questions about the cohesiveness of eighteenth-century New England communities which this study will explore.

Second, my earlier research acquainted me with Lawrence D. Geller and Peter J. Gomes, who were at the time the director and librarian, respectively, of Pilgrim Hall in Plymouth. In many conversations, they argued that Plymouth County, which I had unreflectively viewed as a social and economic backwater, exhibited an eighteenth- and early nineteenth-century pattern of development that may not have differed markedly from the pattern of most of New England. I am indebted to them for convincing me that, whatever the precise weight of their arguments might be, Plymouth County merits serious scholarly study.

I am, of course, also indebted to many others. Research was financed by a grant from the National Science Foundation, grant number SOC 76-14338 A01, which was supplemented with research funds provided by the Yale Law School. Any opinions and conclusions expressed in the book, however, are those of the author and do not necessarily reflect the views of the foundation. Research funds were administered by Emily Golia.

Several people provided secretarial assistance. Carole Bonner typed the final draft of the manuscript. Muneera Spence drew the map of Plymouth County. Jean Doherty and Barbara Perry coordinated the work of many others who performed lesser secretarial chores. I am indebted to the Dyer Memorial Library, the Hilles Library of the Andover Newton Theological Seminary, the Massachusetts Historical Society, and the Rhode Island Historical Society for permission to publish excerpts from their collections. Douglas Jones kindly gave permission to read and cite his Ph.D. dissertation. Evelyn C. Coughlin, Barbara Delorey, Manfred Kohl, Robert Pardon, Oren A. Peterson, David Ripple, Marshall W. Ross, Hilda Stenbeck, Leonard H. Smith, and Leah Warburton graciously facilitated research in local church records. Michael Glazier generously permitted me to retain the copyright on an earlier version of this book so that it could be published here.

John W. Reifenberg gathered, analyzed, and checked statistical data from the court records. Bruce A. Ackerman, Robert A. Burt, Robert M. Cover, Robert A. Gross, Adam J. Hirsch, Leon S. Lipson, Jerry L. Mashaw, and Edmund S. Morgan read and criticized various drafts of the book. David Thomas Konig, who read several drafts and discussed them with me on innumerable occasions, provided invaluable ideas and bibliographical guidance as well as useful criticism.

The communities of eighteenth-century Plymouth County have special meaning to me as societies where people never forgot the basic facts of human existence: on the one hand, their mortal nature and their limited capacity to apprehend mankind's place in the scheme of things; and, on the other, their power to generate new life and new ideas. The late Myra R. Brunswick, who during the course of her terminal illness typed all but the final draft of this book, brought home through her courage and fortitude some of the sad, though significant, lessons that can be learned from eighteenth-century Plymouth. At the same time, my family always provided joy. Leila's exuberance made daily living fun throughout my work on this book, just as Gregory does today. My wife, Elaine, never forgot life's difficult but most rewarding tasks.

The people of eighteenth-century Plymouth lived with basics ultimately as tillers of the soil. Thus, they knew that, if a field is to produce crops, it is more important to plow and sow it seasonably than to do so perfectly but too late. Like the farmers of Plymouth, I am quite aware that I have not plowed my field as exhaustively or as perfectly as it might be plowed. But I have plowed it seasonably and, I hope, well enough so that it will lead to new and fruitful ideas.

W. E. N.

Guilford, Conn.
January 1980

Dispute and Conflict Resolution in Plymouth County, Massachusetts, 1725–1825

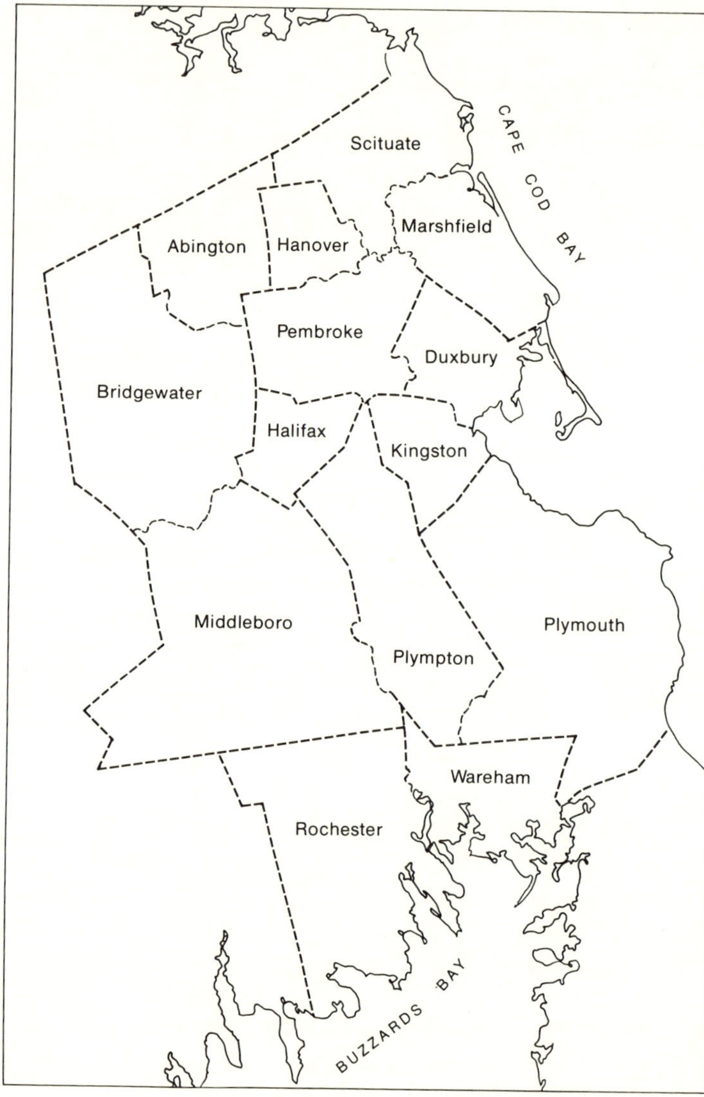

CAPE COD BAY
Scituate
Marshfield
Abington
Hanover
Pembroke
Duxbury
Bridgewater
Halifax
Kingston
Middleboro
Plympton
Plymouth
Wareham
Rochester
BUZZARDS BAY

1 Introduction: The Larger Context of Conflict and Dispute

For more than a decade, historians have engaged in an often acrimonious debate about the character of eighteenth-century New England communities. On the one hand, these communities have been described as peaceable kingdoms governed by a widely shared consensus of ethical values.[1] At the other extreme, several scholars have demonstrated that groups and classes in eighteenth-century New England often became embroiled in disputes with each other.[2] They have also argued that those disputes were resolved when groups enjoying access to power imposed their will on those lacking such access.[3] This debate is a significant one that poses grave implications for a number of issues in early American history.

But the debate has focused on the wrong question in asking how disputatious New Englanders were. There is no doubt whatever that conflict existed and that disputes arose in eighteenth-century Massachusetts.[4] But this does not mean that people who lived in the eighteenth century were unusually disputatious. In order to determine that they were—or, indeed, that they were not—it would be essential to know not only the frequency at which disputes arose in the eighteenth century, but also the frequency at which they arose in other cultures at other times. Then, it might be possible to know whether eighteenth-century New England manifested a typical rate of conflict, an unusually high rate, or a low rate. In the absence of data from other cultures and of criteria for comparison of such data, however, all that can be known is that disputes did arise in provincial Massachusetts.

Because it is not possible to determine how disputatious eighteenth-century New England was, this study will focus upon the techniques by which disputes were resolved rather than upon the frequency at which they arose. Two typologies of dispute resolution will emerge for the communities under study. It will appear that some communities were able to resolve most disputes between their residents without recourse to outside institutions, such as courts. In other communities, however, disputants frequently did turn to the courts. These two types of communities will be examined and compared in detail in an effort to isolate the factors that either facilitated or impeded communitarian dispute resolution.

I hope such a comparative analysis will shed some light on the character of New England communities, at least in reference to the single locality that is being analyzed: Plymouth County, Massachusetts, during the period 1725–1825. The first step in the analysis will be to identify the three principal institutions—the town meeting, the church congregation, and the courts of law—to which conflicts and disputes could be taken; to determine the types of cases over which each institution had jurisdiction; and to study the procedures by which each functioned. The second step will be to identify communities during the period 1725–74 in which the town meeting and the church congregation resolved most conflicts and to compare them with communities in which conflicts were frequently taken to the county courts. The third step will be to compare litigation statistics for the period 1781–1825, when cases were taken more frequently to courts, with statistics already presented for the period 1725–74. The final step will be to discuss the factors that underlie the different litigation rates and thereby specify the characteristics that made some eighteenth-century communities capable of resolving disputes through their own local institutions.

Before beginning the analysis, I would like to provide some background information about Plymouth County and its towns.

In 1685, when the old Plymouth Colony was merged into the Dominion of New England and Plymouth County was first established, the county consisted of seven towns,[5] including the town of Plymouth, the first permanent European settlement in New England and the second permanent English settlement on the North American continent. An eighth town, Rochester, was transferred from Barnstable to Plymouth County in 1707. Six new towns were established between 1707 and 1739,[6] but, thereafter, except for Carver, which was created in 1790, no new towns were incorporated until 1820.[7] In that and the following three years, four towns were incorporated.[8] The map on page 2 shows the towns in the county between 1739 and 1790, the longest period of time in which no new ones were established.

According to a 1690 census, the largest town in the county was Scituate, which had an estimated population of 865 people, followed by Plymouth with 775, Bridgewater with 440, Duxbury with 410, Marshfield with 400, and Middleboro with 165.[9] However, by the time of the next census, in 1765, Scituate had fallen to third and Plymouth to fourth place. In that year, the largest town in the county was Bridgewater. Its 3,924 inhabitants made it the fifth largest town in the entire colony.[10] Middleboro, with 3,412 inhabitants, was the second largest town in the county and the eighth largest in the colony. Then came Scituate and Plymouth, whose populations were 2,488 and 2,177, respectively. The population of the remaining towns is given in table 1.1. The total population of the county was 23,119.[11]

The first federal census in 1790 showed a general pattern of growth among the county's towns, but no striking changes in their rankings. Bridgewater, whose population was 4,975, remained the largest town in the county and the fifth largest in the state. Middleboro, with 4,526 inhabitants, continued as the second largest town in the county and tenth largest in the state. Its population of 2,995 moved Plymouth into third place while Scituate dropped to fourth with a population of 2,856. The populations of other towns are listed in table 1.1. The county's population had grown to 29,535, an increase of 28 percent.

By the 1820 census, however, some major changes were becoming visible. Bridgewater, with 5,670 residents, remained the largest town in the county, but slipped to sixth largest in the state. Middleboro remained the second largest town, with a population of 4,687, but its rate of growth slowed significantly: over a thirty-year period it gained a mere 161 inhabitants. Plymouth, on the other hand, enjoyed substantial growth, its population rising from 2,995 to 4,348. As shown in table 1.1, several other towns in the county also enjoyed significant growth between 1790 and 1820. During these years, the county's total population increased to 35,107, a gain of 19 percent.

During the eighteenth century, the people of Plymouth County engaged predominantly in agricultural pursuits. Census figures for 1765 demonstrate that, except for Plymouth, the largest towns in the county tended to be geographically extensive entities characterized by agrarian economies. For example, the two towns having the largest populations in 1765—Bridgewater and Middleboro—were also those encompassing the largest areas. The economies of both towns

TABLE 1.1 Population of Plymouth County Towns, 1765, 1790, and 1820

	1765	*1790*	*1820*
Bridgewater	3,942	4,975	5,670
Middleboro	3,412	4,526	4,687
Scituate	2,488	2,856	3,305
Plymouth	2,177	2,995	4,348
Rochester	1,939	2,644	3,034
Pembroke	1,409	1,954	2,214
Plympton	1,390	1,803	930
Carver	—	—	839
Abington	1,263	1,453	1,920
Marshfield	1,147	1,269	1,532
Hanover	1,084	1,084	1,211
Duxbury	1,050	1,454	2,403
Kingston	759	1,004	1,313
Halifax	556	664	749
Wareham	503	854	952
Total	23,119	29,535	35,107

were heavily agricultural.[12] Few residents engaged directly in commercial pursuits, and manufacturing enterprises tended to be small-scale ones like gristmills and sawmills that were subsidiary to agricultural pursuits.[13] However, Middleboro did have an extensive iron-mining and manufacturing industry, and Bridgewater was a center for the manufacture of tools and other iron products.[14] Two other interior towns embracing relatively large, fertile areas—Pembroke and Plympton—were also among the larger towns in the county. They ranked sixth and seventh in population, respectively.[15] All these towns, it should be noted, had grown substantially since the census of

1690. Bridgewater had grown about nine times; Middleboro, about twenty; and Pembroke and Plympton had not even existed as separate towns in the seventeenth century.

In contrast, towns along the coast that did not have extensive agricultural hinterlands and were dependent upon commerce and maritime pursuits remained small and, one can almost say, stagnant during the provincial period. Four of the six least populous towns in the county—Duxbury, Kingston, Marshfield, and Wareham—were geographically compact entities lying on the coast. Marshfield, the most populous, had been almost as large as Bridgewater in 1689, but by 1765 had fallen to about a fourth of Bridgewater's size. The only nonagrarian coastal town of size and importance in the mid-eighteenth century was Plymouth itself, which was the political and historic as well as the commercial center of the county. Two other towns along the coast, Scituate and Rochester, were the third and fifth largest towns in the county, respectively, but both contained extensive inland areas[16] that probably supported at least half of their residents in agricultural pursuits. In short, if it is assumed that most people living in inland towns engaged in or were dependent upon agriculture for a living and that most of the inhabitants of the coastal towns, including Plymouth, earned their living from commerce, from manufacturing or from the sea, with the populations of Scituate and Rochester divided between those two general categories, an informed though necessarily imprecise guess can be made that more than two-thirds of the county's inhabitants earned their living principally by farming.

As already noted, during the period between 1765 and the first federal census in 1790, population growth was substantial, but no significant change took place in the relative positions of the economically different sorts of towns. The coastal towns, aside from Plymouth, grew at a rate of 28 percent, while the inland agrarian towns grew at the slightly lower rate of 26 percent. Even the town of Plymouth's growth rate—38 percent—was not dramatically out of line with that experienced by the rest of the county. Accordingly, it seems appropriate to assume that as late as 1790 agriculture remained the mainstay of the county's economy.

The next three decades—from 1790 to 1820—brought dramatic economic change. During that period, the population of the coastal towns grew by 29 percent, while the growth rate of the inland towns slowed to 11 percent. To the extent that the coastal towns were more commercial than those of the interior, it is apparent that commercial pursuits were gaining ground in comparison with agriculture, which was laboring under the burden of competition with newly opened lands in the west. Moreover, nonstatistical evidence suggests that the residents of the inland towns, notably Bridgewater and Middleboro, were beginning to turn away from agriculture and toward manufacturing and commerce in order to gain their livelihoods.

It is known, for example, that the first retail mercantile establishments in North Bridgewater were founded during the thirty years between 1790 and 1820[17] and that in 1818 the entire town of Bridgewater possessed three forges, two slitting-mills, two anchor shops, four trip-hammers, three nail factories, and one air furnace.[18] In Middleboro, two cotton factories apparently were established before 1820—one around 1810 and the other in 1813 or 1814—and several trading firms were founded at about the same time.[19] Parallel developments occurred in the smaller towns. In Pembroke, for example, retail business seems to have been conducted at the time of the Revolution by the local innkeeper. This pattern prevailed into the 1790s, when a migrant from Plymouth opened a new retail establishment, and, a few years later, erected what was apparently the first building in town other than the meetinghouse that did not also serve as a residence; he later became the local postmaster.[20] Although little is known about retailing in Plympton, it is known that a cotton factory was built there in 1813 and that a blast furnace had been constructed even earlier, in 1794, in nearby Carver.[21]

In summary, a survey of the economy of Plymouth County over the course of the eighteenth and early nineteenth centuries reveals an initial period of rapid agricultural growth concentrated primarily in large inland towns like Bridgewater, Middleboro, Pembroke, and Plympton. After 1790, however, this growth ceased, and towns dependent solely upon agriculture for their livelihood stagnated. As a result, population growth in the county as a whole also slowed down. In several towns, however, first commerce and maritime industries and then manufacturing assumed increasing prominence. Those towns continued to grow, sometimes with amazing speed. In all of this, Plymouth County developed in the same direction, although perhaps not as rapidly as the rest of Massachusetts and New England, except for its failure to produce a major metropolitan center such as Boston, to the north, or Providence, to the west.[22]

However, in another respect—namely, its religious diversity—eighteenth-century Plymouth County was quite different from most of Massachusetts. Plymouth first manifested its greater toleration of religious dissent in 1661, while it was still a separate colony. In that year, the town of Scituate granted asylum to several Quakers who had been expelled from Boston under pain of death.[23] Thereafter, several towns in the county became havens for Quakers, and by the eighteenth century two Quaker meetings had been established in the county, in Pembroke and Rochester.[24] After the Great Awakening, another town, Middleboro, became the center of the Baptist movement in Massachusetts under the leadership of Isaac Backus, the elder of the first Baptist church in that town.[25] Following the American Revolution, religious dissent became even more widespread in Plymouth County. But, as dissent spread in most of the rest of the state, Plymouth's pattern of religious diversity became little different from patterns elsewhere in Massachusetts.

The formal legal system of Plymouth County, on the other hand, never varied significantly from that of Massachusetts as a whole. Legal uniformity was minimally insured because the highest court, known as the Superior Court in the provincial period and renamed the Supreme Judicial Court by the constitution of 1780, rode circuit around the entire state and heard a large number of appeals from the lower courts in every county. Previous research into eighteenth- and nineteenth-century Massachusetts law[26] has convinced me that there was no noticeable variation in the jurisdictional, procedural, and substantive rules applied by the judiciary in different counties. I do not propose, however, to document this conclusion in the remainder of this book.

Instead, I propose to turn to an analysis of one aspect of the social function of law in eighteenth- and early nineteenth-century Massachusetts. More specifically I shall inquire into the changing role of the courts as one set of institutions which, together with town meetings and churches, were available to hear disputes between people living within the county. After an initial discussion in the next chapter of how dispute resolution worked in each of the three available institutions, I shall present a statistical analysis addressed to the question of why disputants selected one institution in preference to another. Let me note preliminarily that it is possible to identify some towns in which at certain times comparatively few such disputes were brought to court, while it is equally possible to identify other towns at other times that produced a great deal of litigation. The methodology employed in the following chapters will be to compare the times and places in which litigation was frequent with those in which it was rare in an effort to identify some other differences that may help explain why disputants preferred courts to other institutions or other institutions to courts. I will postpone to the final chapter the presentation of an hypothesis that explains why the differences upon which I focus may account for the differing preferences. Because research of this sort has not been done in the past, we cannot, of course, know the extent to which the pattern that will be revealed in Plymouth will conform to patterns elsewhere in New England.

2 The Institutions for Dispute Resolution: Town, Court, and Church, 1725–1774

It is difficult to imagine how any society could exist if all disputes between individuals were taken for resolution to formal institutions. Everyday experience suggests, for example, that many disputes arise and are settled within the family, however much the nature of the family may vary from one society to another. Similarly, people dealing with each other on an ongoing though less intimate basis often resolve disputes by compromises designed to keep their relationships intact. In fact, the need to maintain social relationships limits human capacity for disputation even more pervasively by equipping people with often unarticulated assumptions about their rights vis-à-vis the rights of others. These assumptions prevent them from even seeing many issues that could be raised to the level of open disputes were they inclined so to raise them. Finally, it is not uncommon for a mutual acquaintance of two people engaged in a dispute to offer or to be requested to render aid in mediating it.

Although processes such as these may have been essential to community life in eighteenth-century Plymouth, there is little that the historian, who must rely on written records for evidence of social practice, can say about them. The difficulty, of course, is that informal processes of dispute resolution, because of their very informality, do not often result in the production of written records. Hence, the historian can obtain only occasional glimpses of the manner in which such processes functioned in the past. Eighteenth-century court records indicate, for instance, that some cases brought to court were ultimately settled by the intervention of impartial referees,[1] and that other cases came to court only after they had been submitted to impartial arbitration and one of the disputants had refused to abide by the arbitrators' award.[2] Occasional nonjudicial records show parties, without court intervention, leaving disputes "to Indeferent men mutually Chosen by them."[3] Beyond this, however, the written record is silent.

Accordingly, the historian interested in dispute resolution must study formal institutions. In eighteenth-century Plymouth, there were three categories of institutions which, because of their central importance to the ongoing life of the county, might be expected to have been deeply involved in adjudicating disputes. These were the towns, the courts, and the churches.

The Town

The towns functioned primarily as agencies of government and intervened routinely only in cases of group as distinguished, however imprecisely, from cases of individual conflict. In Rochester, for example, a town meeting was called in 1722 "to Consult Wheather the Town will pay" the taxes due from Quakers for the support of the Congregationalist minister.[4] In the end, however, the broad issue of dissenters' liability to religious taxation was settled by provincial legislation enacted partly in response to pressure from London. A similar issue came before the town meetings at Duxbury and Kingston in 1745—whether "to allow itinerant preachers to preach in the meetinghouse."[5] Kingston voted not to allow itinerants,[6] while in Duxbury the town meeting "finding much difficulty and having had a long debate about the above said business brought nothing to a vote."[7] The disposition of town funds was another troublesome issue. In 1726, for example, there was "much uneasiness" in Plymouth relating to the division of school funds among different parts of the town.[8] Another issue that generated widespread conflict—fishing rights—was commonly dealt with by the enactment of bylaws "for the more orderly & Regular taking of said fish and for the preventing the unreasonable wasteing and destroying of them."[9] Finally, conflict was anticipated and provision made "to take care of the indians and negroes that on ye Sabbath-day they resort to those seats which are built for them in said meeting-house" as well as "to take care and to suppress those youths that are vicious or disorderly on Sabbath-days."[10]

Towns also dealt, however, with special categories of disputes between individuals that were related to the towns' governmental jurisdiction. Private interests often collided in the determination of road routes. In Halifax, for instance, the town meeting in effect resolved a private conflict when it refused to build a bridge "for the Convenience of William Holmes in going to meeting," in part because "a Bridge there will prove Detrimental to Several persons who have petitioned against it."[11] Private rights were also involved when a town considered requests for permission to construct mills and dams or otherwise to use the town's streams. Thus, the Plymouth town meeting authorized construction of a distillery adjacent to the town pond only after finding it "a Place suitable & Convenient For that Purpose."[12] Normally, permission to construct a dam or mill was granted "under the Inspection Restriction & Regulation of the Town,"[13] and hence it was appropriate for "Divers people" to complain to the town if "they sufered Wrong by the Ill grinding their corn by a child That had not Descresion to Doe what Was just between man & man."[14] The continuing supervisory powers of towns also led to individual requests for redeterminations of the precise scope of grants. One such case in Middleboro dragged on for seven years. It began in 1764, when the town meeting was asked whether "the Mill Taile Called Bennets mill be any part of the Old Stone ware So called in Nemasket River in Said Town," and did not end until 1770, when a committee appointed to "Discribe the Limits of the old Stone wair so Called on Nemasket River" found "that the tail of William Bennetts Grist Mill doth not Belong to said Old Stone wair."[15]

Likewise, the powers of towns to protect public health required them to hear claims such as "ye Petition of William Sergeant Desireing the Town will Consider & allow him for Damages he sustained by Removeing his Family & Business, by Reason of the Small Pox"[16] and "the Affair of Abigail Bartlett & Isaac Morton Respecting their Loss & Damages They sustained By Perez Tilson's Haveing the Small Pox in their House."[17] In such matters, the town meeting apparently undertook to adjudicate private rights, for in Sergeant's case the Plymouth town meeting directed its selectmen to determine "whether ye Town must pay his Damages, or ye persons by Reason of whom he was put to ye Trouble & Costs."[18] A final sort of private dispute over which towns, by virtue of both legislation and long-standing custom, had jurisdiction concerned disagreements between neighbors about their obligations to maintain fences; here the town's fence viewers had authority to divide the burden of maintaining a fence between neighbors "in Equil half."[19]

In addition to adjudicating disputes between private individuals, towns were often parties to disputes. These cases could be of almost any sort, although two types were most common: disputes between towns and their ministers[20] and disputes between towns and alleged trespassers upon town lands.[21] Occasionally, towns attempted to adjudicate these cases themselves, as when the Marshfield town meeting voted that, if the claimant of a cow that was also claimed by the town "Should Refuse to Leave it to men," the town's agents should act "as if sd Cow was their own."[22] Similarly, a Pembroke meeting decided upon a "Complaint made to this Town" that, if a holder of a right to build a pew in the meetinghouse did not forthwith pay money owed to the town for the pew, the town would "proceed to make disposition of ye sd. priviledg."[23] Normally, though, towns recognized the ultimate jurisdiction of the courts over their disputes with private parties, as did Scituate when it voted to "bring a Writt of Ejectment" against an alleged trespasser.[24] Plympton did the same when it appointed an agent to demand town records in possession of a former town clerk and "upon his refusing to deliver the said Town Books and papers, to prosecute him in the law."[25]

In dealing with disputes involving private individuals, towns often employed procedures in many respects analogous to those of the courts. Matters were almost always brought to a town's attention by a private petition or complaint, after which the adverse party was given "timely Notice to attend" a proceeding at which his rights and obligations would be determined.[26] On one occasion, when a complainant was not present, his matter "was dismist for ye present Meeting,"[27] but typically when both adversaries were present their contentions were heard.[28] Sometimes witnesses were even permitted to give more formal testimony.[29] As in the courts, it appears to have been inappropriate for "Relations" of a party to play a determinative role in town proceedings, apparently out of a concern that their interest might overwhelm their judgment.[30]

Even when issues of broader public concern were being considered, traces of judicial procedure found their way into town practice. In public as well as private disputes, it was essential that the parties thereto be present at the town meeting. Thus, the town of Plymouth "thought it best to adjourn" a meeting that had been called to determine the location of the town's schools, "[i]t being a stormy day and a very difficult Time to travel [and] The Inhabitants of ye Town in ye Second Precinct and at ye Eel River and ye North part of ye Town not Being at ye Meeting."[31] Similarly, in Rochester a meeting was called to reconsider a vote to increase the minister's salary which had been taken at a meeting that had been "Thin[ly]" attended; it was hoped that "the Mater" would "be fa[i]rly tried" at the second meeting.[32] It was also essential for the town to be adequately notified of matters to be presented at a meeting and for issues to be presented to the voters in a form they could comprehend. Thus, a Plympton meeting was adjourned when "an objection" was "raised against the legality of the said meeting" because of some unspecified defect in the warrant by which it had been called,[33] while in Middleboro a matter was put to a second vote when "a Number of Persons" indicated that "they Did not understand" the issue as it had initially been posed.[34]

It was important to obtain the full participation of town residents in meetings because many issues were incapable of definitive resolution unless nearly all residents acquiesced in a meeting's outcome. One such issue arose during 1725 and 1726 in the town of Plymouth, where the sale of some town land had generated a fund for the support of schools. Residents of the north and south ends of the town wanted part of the fund used for the maintenance of schools in their localities rather than for a single school in the town center. After "a Considerable debate," a motion that the division of the money "be left to Indifferent men" was defeated, and the residents of the town center put through a motion that the entire fund be devoted "to the use & maintenance of a Grammar School within the Town of Plymouth for the use of the whole Town."[35] But this vote did not end the matter because residents of the north and south ends would not acquiesce in it. Apparently they submitted petitions both to the town meeting and to the General Court seeking to have the vote reversed,[36] perhaps arguing as did some Bridgewater petitioners in a similar dispute a decade later that those institutions should "not be governed by numbers but by reason and justice."[37] In any event, "the Devision of ye Town" resulting from the minority's persistence produced "much uneasiness." Within several months, "the matter was moved to the Town about an accomedation" and the town appointed a committee that drafted a compromise plan.[38]

A similar dispute, between the inhabitants of the northern and southern parts of town occurred in Plympton in the early 1730s. The dispute began when residents of the northern sector, in which the town church was located, voted to have a second minister appointed to share the pulpit with the existing minister. Residents of the southern sector protested that having two ministers in one meetinghouse would constitute "an unreasonable charge."[39] Preferring to establish a second church in the southern part of town, they petitioned for the creation of a separate southern parish, observing that they had done their "duty in times past in supporting the minister here settled, but now think it our duty to settle a minister amongst ourselves." They also argued that the northern sector's call of a second minister was "not agreeable either to

Scripture Rule or the practice of Churches" and was "a great imposition upon us."[40] Although the majority of the town opposed the petition,[41] the General Court nonetheless created the southern sector into a separate parish. But even this did not end the dispute. The south parish now petitioned to become a separate town, and a committee appointed by the town to treat with the parish reported that "they could not agree upon any thing."[42] A year later, however, the difference was accommodated when the south parish abandoned its drive for independence and in return received an exemption from school taxes on condition that it maintain its own school.[43]

Probably the most significant issue on which general acquiescence was vital in the mid-eighteenth century was the choice of town ministers. Town meetings, or in larger towns that were subdivided into parishes, parish meetings, had to concur in the choice. When ministers found themselves confronted with "dissatisfied Brethren" who in large numbers entered their dissent to town proceedings relating either to the church or to the ministry,[44] "the Difficulties" that attended their "Continuance In the Work of the ministry" often led them to seek dismissal from their posts.[45] Thus, in Halifax, where some residents in the mid-1760s were "uneasy with" the incumbent minister, he decided not to continue in his post even though the town had indicated by a vote of 19–14 that it wished him to remain.[46] In Hanover, the minister resigned when the town voted his salary "by a majority of one in the number Sixty-five but Could not get a Vote for the towns to be assest for the money."[47] Similarly, the minister of Kingston resigned when a committee elected by a majority of the town barred him from inviting the Reverend George Whitefield to speak by locking the church doors.[48] In view of the difficulties to which divisions in a community could lead, it is not surprising that ministers hesitated to accept calls in which only a majority of the town had concurred[49] or that towns seeking to obtain the services of a minister strove to make their choice "by a unanimous vote"[50] or even "a very unanimous vote."[51] Indeed, after a protracted dispute over the choice of a minister, most men in the Mattapoisett parish entered into a covenant "that we will Desist all our Differences in the precinct affairs," that they "shall be buried In Oblivion & that we will unite for the Calling of an orderly minister."[52]

In short, powerful pressures often induced town residents who attended meetings not "to proceed from a Disposition to Stur up Domestick Disturbances."[53] On the contrary, towns hoped that "no Intrested Disputes may make any breach of Union,"[54] so that the town could "advise and agree upon . . . measures"[55] and thereby obtain "Love and Unity [and] Peace."[56] Of course, towns could not always obtain unanimity, and certain sorts of matters, notably the election of officials, were often determined by majority vote.[57] Nevertheless, many towns recognized the futility of attempting to resolve all conflict by a majority vote, and, if they could not obtain a resolution by consensus, simply took no vote at all. When Duxbury, for example, was considering whether to exclude itinerant preachers from its meetinghouse, "the said town finding much difficulty and having had a long debate about the above said business brought nothing to a vote."[58] Similarly, in a debate concerning a bridge within the town, the residents of Bridgewater "discoursed of ye matter & did not think propper to pass any vote in that afair."[59] And, on at least three occasions in Marshfield, "many things" were "debated and discoursed of in pursuance of the warrant, . . . but nothing put to a vote."[60]

Because town clerks often failed to specify whether votes were taken unanimously or by mere majority vote, the extent of unanimity in eighteenth-century Plymouth County towns can never be known. We can speculate, however, that votes of a mere majority were not often useful devises for bringing to final resolution disputes in which a minority was unwilling to abide by the majority's will: the town records contain many instances in which a minority was able to keep a dispute alive until the majority came to an accommodation, and they also show a hesitancy on the part of town leaders to bring unresolved disputes to a vote. It is possible to talk with even greater confidence about the kinds of issues that came before towns. The town meeting was essentially a political body that dealt with matters of general community concern which rarely produced open contention among competing groups within a town. Except for the fence cases, disputes between individuals came before the meetings only if they arose out of prior municipal activity such as the building of roads, mills, and the like. In sum, the town meeting was not a prominent institution for adjudicating disputes. Although a few cases were heard there, town meetings resolved only a small portion of the disputes that arose among their residents.

The Courts

More central to the dispute-resolution process were the courts. Like other counties in eighteenth-century Massachusetts, Plymouth had a complex hierarchy of judicial institutions.[61] At the base of the hierarchy were the one-man courts of the justices of the peace, which had jurisdiction over minor civil actions and petty criminal offenses. Appeal lay from the justices to the Inferior Court of Common Pleas in civil cases and to the Court of General Sessions of the Peace in criminal cases; on appeal, the parties received a trial *de novo*. Inasmuch as no justices' records survive for eighteenth-century Plymouth, it is impossible to describe the actual work of the justices as distinguished from their jurisdiction.

The next court was General Sessions, which was composed of all the county's justices of the peace. Sessions had a broad administrative jurisdiction, pursuant to which it approved the establishment and alteration of county roads and bridges, granted licenses, approved town bylaws, supervised poor-law administration, and controlled county fiscal matters. The Plymouth Court of Sessions also exercised legislative power when it adopted a regulation to prevent stench from mussels on a beach.[62] Finally, it possessed jurisdiction over all criminal offenses except a few especially serious crimes reserved for the Superior Court. Most of the criminal prosecutions that were brought within the county were for morals offenses. Prosecutions for fornication, for example, amounted to 28 percent of all criminal cases, and other sex offenses, including paternity, constituted 4 percent of all cases. Fifteen percent of all prosecutions were for breach of the Sabbath, and another 3 percent were for profane speech. The next largest category of prosecutions were those for violent crimes, which accounted for 15 percent of all cases. Seven percent of all prosecutions were for theft; another 7 percent were for liquor violations; and a final 7 percent were for refusals to serve in office. Miscellaneous offenses also added up to 7 percent of all cases, and the nature of the offense was unspecified in 8 percent of the cases.[63]

Sitting alongside General Sessions was the Inferior Court of Common Pleas. Like General Sessions, the Inferior Court normally met quarterly in the town of Plymouth, the county seat. The Inferior Court possessed original jurisdiction over all civil suits except petty cases heard before a single justice of the peace and cases in which the crown was plaintiff. Seventy-four percent of all the cases heard during the period 1725–74 were actions between private individuals for the collection of debts. More specifically, 36 percent of all cases were actions of case on notes; 23 percent were actions of debt on bonds; 15 percent were actions of case on accounts; and 0.4 percent were actions to foreclose mortgages. Land disputes constituted 4 percent of all litigation; suits for nondelivery of goods constituted 4 percent; defamation actions and actions for the recovery of wages each constituted 1 percent; and various miscellaneous actions in combination amounted to 4 percent. In 13 percent of all cases, the description of the form of action was too general to permit classification.[64]

Appeal lay from both General Sessions and the Inferior Court of Common Pleas to the Superior Court of Judicature, Assize, and General Jail Delivery, where the parties received a trial *de novo*. The Superior Court possessed original jurisdiction in a few categories of cases, but nearly all the cases it heard were on appeal from the two lower courts. This court, which rode circuit throughout the Province of Massachusetts Bay, usually came to Plymouth County only once each year.

In criminal cases tried in General Sessions and in all cases tried in the Inferior and the Superior courts, litigants enjoyed the right to trial by jury.[65] In the early part of the eighteenth century, jurors were elected for each court term by town meetings in each town in the county, but in mid-century, the General Court, fearing that towns might elect jurors sympathetic to particular litigants, required them to draw jurors by lot from previously compiled lists of town residents eligible for jury duty.[66] This statutory change did not, however, deprive towns of their ability to determine who served on juries in general, though it did prevent them from naming particular persons to a certain jury. Town meetings preserved their power because, when lists of eligible jurors were presented to them, they "then by Vote Selected out of the List laid before them . . .

Such as they Judged most Suitable to Serve as Jurors."[67] As a result, jurors who were ultimately selected for service by lot were only those previously found acceptable to the towns.

Despite town control over the jury-selection process, juries appear to have represented a fair cross section of the voting population of the county. The only voters who appear to have been systematically excluded from jury service were religious dissenters who did not attend services of the Congregational church. In fact, of the 1,613 different men who served on juries in Plymouth County from 1748 to 1774,[68] only 43,[69] or less than 3 percent, can be identified as having at any time in their lives joined a dissenting congregation. The absence of other discriminatory exclusions in the jury-selection process is not surprising because jury duty in eighteenth-century Plymouth County, like such duty today, was undoubtedly a tedious chore involving travel to the county seat that most men would prefer to avoid. Hence, towns that were choosing men for jury duty must often have found themselves in a position of needing to conscript jurors for service rather than being able to exclude those eager to serve. Whatever the details of the selection process, it appears that approximately 28 percent of all adult males in the county served on juries.[70]

Once juries were assembled in court, they exerted immense power over the outcome of cases. Basic court procedures, such as the requirements that litigants be given notice of proceedings and an opportunity to be heard, were followed in eighteenth-century Plymouth courts,[71] but eighteenth-century juries, unlike juries today, had effective power to determine the law involved in the cases before them as well as the facts. Their power resulted from litigants' practice of generally presenting mixed questions of law and fact to juries; from the frequent failure of judges to deliver a detailed and unambiguous set of instructions on the law; and from the rule that, even if such instructions were delivered, a jury verdict contrary thereto could not be set aside.[72]

Thus, the courts, which were the principal nonecclesiastical institution for the settlement of conflict and disputes, were not entirely separate from the towns. The main link between them was, of course, the jury, a body of town nominees possessing ultimate decisional power in the judicial process. Courts and towns also followed similar procedures of requiring persons interested in proceedings to be notified of them and to be given an opportunity to be heard; both institutions also tended to exclude interested persons from participation in the final decisional processes by which disputes were resolved. The primary difference between the two was in their jurisdiction. The task of the towns was political governance, and, in general, they resolved only those disputes that came to them in the process of governance. On the other hand, the main function of the courts was dispute resolution, even though the Court of Sessions, in particular, did possess some broader governmental jurisdiction.

The Church

Like the courts, the third institution that resolved disputes—the church—heard a wide variety of cases, at least in the five decades before the War of Independence. Many were analogous to criminal prosecutions in the courts of law. Churches proceeded, for example, against individuals guilty of fornication, breaches of the Sabbath, and drunkenness[73]—offenses that were also the subject of frequent prosecutions by civil authorities.[74] Proceedings were brought against both men and women for fornication. In Plymouth, there were seventeen such cases between 1730 and 1770.[75] Similarly, the records of the Fourth Church of Bridgewater reported some nineteen cases between 1737, when the records began, and the outbreak of the Revolution.[76] All nineteen of these entries took the form of the first one, which reported that "Isaac Kingman & wife made a public acknowledgment for ye Sin of fornication"[77]—that is, for giving birth to a child less than nine months after their marriage. Similar entries also appear in the records of other churches.[78] Women committing the sin of fornication with men who did not subsequently become their husbands were also subjected to ecclesiastical disciplinary proceedings,[79] as were men who did not later marry the women with whom they were accused of committing the sin.[80] One of the disciplinary proceedings against a single woman was further complicated by her "Speaking falsely & Sinfully about it; Particularly in Saying, that if She was with Child, it was hers, & no bodyes else; and in Calling her maker to witness in discoursing on the affair."[81]

Other sorts of sexual misconduct were also subject to church discipline. A serious case involving polygamy arose in Wareham. It began in 1747 when Lydia Bump, who had "for some considerable time past kept company with" Eleazer King, became "published to" him "in order for marriage: altho her husband has not been absent but about one year & half," and the General Court had refused to grant Lydia a divorce because "nothing appeared to them but that her husband was alive." Eleazer and Lydia were nevertheless wed, for in 1749 Eleazer was debarred from special ordinances with the church because of the marriage. Proceedings did not come to an end until 1751, when, as a result of her husband's absence for a term of four years, it became lawful for Lydia to marry Eleazer and she thereupon confessed her guilt of "the sin of Poligemy," for her "too hasty proceeding."[82]

There were also lesser cases of indecency. For example, Robert Washburn of Titicut was punished for the sin of "entertaining a spirit of carnality."[83] In Wareham, Abigail Muxom and Joseph Benson were reported as having "been seen (by diverse persons) to act toward each other very immodestly & unbecoming married persons," which "caused a great disturbance in his family, especially with his wife, & also . . . opened ye mouths of many to speak reproachfully of our holy religion." Witnesses testified that they had seen the two of them together "talking of balderdash stuff, & kissing & hugging one another in the absence of her husband" and that "their behaviour was uncommon for married people, she fawning about him, & sometimes in his lap, or upon his knee, and he haleing of her, runing his face up to hers, & as we suppose kissing of her, or aiming so to do, & talking and joocking like young people." Abigail denied all these charges, but did admit that she "did several times call her child to her and ask the child who its father was, & the child would answer Doctor Jo's at which she would laugh & make sport of." On the basis of this admission, she was "suspended from our communion till she give Christian satisfaction for this her offence."[84]

Another case arose in Rochester as a result of a "Storey that was gone about" involving Edward Winslow, Jr., and Sarah Doty—"of his desiring to have to do with her In a dishonest way."[85] Because Sarah refused to give evidence against Winslow, the proceeding consisted solely of offers of exculpatory evidence. The following statement by Winslow's wife is typical[86] of those that led to his exculpation:

> [M]y Hond Father Edward Winslow & Doty her husband being present at the same time, My father told her that he had been informed that she had raised or spread a Scandalous Report of his son Edward In saying that he offered incivility to her and would have been dishonest with her. She asked my Father who told him so & my Father did not name them then she said being them, they Dare not

Say so to my face for it is a pernicious lye. Then my Father said to her woman do not clear him because he is my son if he is guilty but let him bare the blame and shame for he is but a man and liable to fall as well as others, Then she replyed & said I never did say any such thing of him & said why should I say any such thing of him for I never had had any reason for it.

Proceedings for breach of the Sabbath were also frequent. In an entry that was frequently duplicated in its own and other church records, the First Church of Rochester sent "a messenger . . . to their Brother Paul Sears To know why he did not attend the Publick worship of God on Sabbath Days no more frequently."[87] A more unusual case arose in Duxbury when Deacon Ezekiel Soul "was charged with breaking the holy Sabbath, in moving a vessel in this harbour, upon that day." He responded that "he was sorry for what he had done inasmuch as it was an occasion of offence, and as many might take occasion thence to vilify religion, and give themselves liberty in profaning the Sabbath, but could not, he said, acknolege that what he had done was in itself immoral" because he believed his conduct fell "under the head of works of necessity."[88] The Soul matter took up three church meetings and was in the end resolved by what appears to be a compromise confession offered by Soul and accepted by the Church, as follows:[89] "Relating to what I did in getting my Sloop out of Island Creek on the Lords day; I then verily thought that ye necessity there then was, made it no Sin. But if it displeased God I am heartily Sorrey for it, and beg his pardon, and of the Chh of & to which I belong forgiveness."

The final persistent offence was drunkenness,[90] a sin into which individuals easily relapsed. Although the records are not fully revealing, it appears that proceedings were brought against an individual only when he was guilty of "sinfull frequent & Continued following of Strong drink"[91] and only after members of the church had "talked with him in order to his reformation: Yet we have no reason to think but that he still lives in the practice of it, to the reproach of religion."[92] The problem of relapses was also reflected in a Halifax case against a Mrs. Bozworth, where "the Church came to a Resolution that if She falls into this sin again (this being ye 2d time of Conviction) they will not immediately receive her upon a confession, But will Suspend her for some time to see whether her Conversation be answerable: and so with Respect to other Relapsers."[93]

In addition to cases involving immorality, the churches of Plymouth County also heard matters that today would likely be classified as torts. On at least one occasion, a church dealt with an incident involving substantial violence, when one Jonathan Justice "ackno'leged his fault in being in a great passion at" one Atwood, in that "he vented himself in Some wicked expressions, &c. and Struck him with a Stone on Ye head."[94] In a companion case, Mary Justice, the wife of Jonathan, "made a Confession of her Sin in giving too great a loose to her passions in a controversy . . . with atwood, & particularly in threatening to beat his Brains out, & in Striking of him."[95] On other occasions, however, churches needed to deal merely with threatening language that never escalated into violence, as when the church in Middleboro concluded "that Brothr *Elnathan Woods* Thretening words to Br David Allen" was "a censurable evil."[96] In other instances, language was adjudged sinful only because it was "offensive and injurious" to the "name" of another.[97] In the Halifax church, Jonathan Drew was found "guilty of Deceit in expressing himself" because he had "wrongfully charged" one man "with lying or false speaking" and had "Spread . . . a false & Scandalous Report" about another's performance of his contract.[98]

In Abington, Captain Hersey was charged with "willfull falsehod" but was found "not guilty."[99] Finally, an individual could also be found guilty of "sinning with his tongue"[100] or of otherwise speaking in a manner "unbecoming a Christian" if he spoke "prophanely by . . . uttering himself in opprobrious speeches & other Vile Terms Before Many people"[101] or if he took "God's name in vain."[102]

Another common tort involved misappropriation of personal property. In Halifax, Jonathan Fuller acknowledged "that he actually took the Stick," described elsewhere in the church's records as "a Cedar Log," "which Jno. Drew Junr. accused him of Stealing," though he claimed "That it was done ignorantly & unwittingly in a great measure (Tho' he had Some Suspitions from the Beginning that it might be Drew's)."[103] The Duxbury church dealt with an offense akin to blackmail, when Elizabeth Sampson confessed that she had "sinfully" threatened to and then did spread "a report" that "Sarah Sampson was with child," with the object of taking from Sarah goods belonging to Sarah's father, "which I touht She had no proper right to Dispose of—She having taken them privately out of her fathers house without his knowledge of or leave for."[104] Meanwhile, in Abington the church punished the fraudulent conduct of Joseph Lincoln, whom it found to have "acted Imprudently & unjustly in buying . . . Turrells Place under a Color to keep off ye Sherrieffe from attaching It."[105] The Abington church also admonished Rioth Sprague for his "sin in the Notorious Breach of ye Eight Commandt" of which he had "been convicted before ye Civile Authority."[106] In Wareham, the church suspended Joseph Bump from special ordinances because he had "of late been publickly convicted of stealing before a Justice Peace by his own confession."[107] Finally, in a case at Rochester the minister of the First Church, Timothy Ruggles, and Deacon Samuel Winslow complained of Noah Sprague, Esquire, that he did

> Enter Into a Stack yard where we had a stack of Salt Hay which we had Purchased of Ezra Bourn Esqr & then & there he did open the Stack of Hay & attempted violently that is Contrary to our leave & against our wills to carry a load of it away Tho we did then produce Several Credible Evidences to wittness that It was ours & contrary to our leave he took of sd Hay & gave it to his cattle & would have carryed away a load of it had he not been prevented by others In which action we apprehend he was guilty of the Scandalous Breach of the Fifth & Eighth Commandments.[108]

Analogous in many ways to this dispute between Ruggles and Sprague were several cases that came before the Wareham and Rochester churches involving title to land. For instance, John Bump informed the Wareham church "by word of mouth that he was offended at ye conduct of his brother Saml. Bump, who . . . had wronged him, by taking and keeping possession of some land & meadow, wh. belonged to him." Upon investigation, it appeared Samuel had obtained a deed to the land in question from his father but had promised neither to record the deed nor to enter the land until his father's death; the land was meanwhile to remain in John's possession and John, in return therefor, was to support his father. The church, accordingly, found Samuel guilty of wrongfully taking the land and suspended him from "their holy communion" until he finally confessed he was "guilty of what is laid in against me," though he added that he "must say (my conscience bearing me witness) that I had his [i.e., his father's] free consent to take possession before ever I did; altho I cant make it appear so plain to the Chh. as I would."[109]

A somewhat analogous case in Rochester involved an accusation that John Winslow had fraudulently surveyed a boundary line when purchasing land from the heirs of Joseph Leavitt so as to induce them to think he was obtaining title to some thirteen acres of their land when he was in fact obtaining title to some twenty-six. Although the church concluded that the complainant "had not made out his charge" against Winslow, the "Pastor & Diverse of ye chh has manifested their uneasiness . . . still Referring to that matter," and accordingly Winslow "ask[ed] their forgiveness."[110] In a third land dispute, this one again in Wareham, Thomas Whetten claimed that he and Thomas Norris had made "a bargain" to divide and "lay out some common land" between them but that Norris had wrongfully taken sole possession of the land. Norris responded that he did "not remember ever making any such bargain," but that, "if I did I have utterly forgot it," and that response was adjudged sufficient "to clear him from ye charge laid in against him."[111]

Other cases were of a contractual nature. One arose upon a complaint before the Abington church against James Lovell "for falsehood & injustice uttered & acted by him Relating to some timber & shingles." The complaint alleged that he had wrongfully taken possession of the timber and shingles; Lovell responded that the goods were his by virtue of a "Bargain" with Joseph Truant, their original owner. Because Lovell could not "prove his Bargain . . . to the Satisfaction of ye Chh," however, he "was Desired to forbore partaking at ye Lords Table till the Matter should be better accomodated."[112] Similarly, in Rochester, Ichabod King accused John Winslow of promising to supply him with "good Tufnails & I paid him his price for such & they were Extremly rotten & now when I tell him of it he says he never promised me such." King further complained about "the wrong" Winslow "did me about the price of some shingles he made for me"—namely, by charging 50 shillings for shingles worth only 30 shillings while "pretend[ing] the stuff was Scarce."[113] Although the Rochester church covenant contained a clause providing that "in all our Dealings with our Neighbour we will have a strict regard to the Rules of Honesty Justice & uprightness that we do not over Reach or Defraud our Neighbour but Endeavor the performance of Relative Dutyes,"[114] the church nonetheless concluded that King "ought to have born as his burden" the injustices done him by Winslow, perhaps because of their trivial nature.[115] In still another case, the Rochester church affirmed an award of arbitrators who had been appointed to resolve a controversy "about the price of some Iron by the reason of Its being poor"[116]—a dispute that in a sense concerned issues of warranty and just price, as did the dispute between Ichabod King and John Winslow.

Arbitration awards, it appears, were routinely enforced by the church, as when Benjamin Fearing was held to have "broken his word & promise" for refusing to abide by an award.[117] Other contractual promises were also frequently enforced. In Middleboro, one member of the church confessed that he had "done Amis—Perticularly yt I have Spoken and Actd Unadvisedly In ye differences wt Some of My Neighbors abt some Eggs & wt others abt ye Ware."[118] Another was punished in Middleboro for "breach of Promise"[119] and a third for "unchristian conduct (particularly his repeated false-speaking & Violation of his Promises)."[120] In Duxbury, yet another man was punished because he had "Spoken falsely by denying that . . . [he] made such a promise" as was laid to him.[121] A final contractual matter to come before Plymouth County churches dealt with an application "for advice with Relation to a difference between" two men "about their accounts."[122]

There is a striking similarity between the dispute-resolution business of Plymouth County churches outlined above and the docket of the county's judiciary. On the criminal side, as related earlier, the main business of the courts was the prosecution and punishment of fornication and other forms of sexual immorality, of Sabbath breaches, and of liquor-law violations. The courts also heard a substantial number of proceedings dealing with theft, on the one hand, and actual or threatened violence, on the other. On the civil side, most of the judiciary's business consisted of disputes over property and contract rights. There was also a smattering of defamation and occasionally other sorts of cases. Unfortunately, it is not possible to speak with statistical precision about ecclesiastical proceedings because record-keeping practices in regard to the resolution of disputes among individuals varied significantly in the different parishes of Plymouth County. In some, a church's adjudication of a controversy was reported in entries saying no more than that "Brother Cobbs case was Dismist June 23, 1741."[123] Still other parishes possess no records at all that reflect ecclesiastical resolution of disputes, perhaps because the records were lost or were never kept or perhaps because some of the churches never adjudicated individual cases. Even parishes that reported disputes extensively kept incomplete records. For instance, an entry in the record book of the First Church of Rochester noted that there were "Many Long & Tedious Cases that have had Their hearing & Determinations That have never been Recorded In the Church Record."[124] Nevertheless, the strong impression that emerges from examination of church files is that the two largest heads of ecclesiastical jurisdiction were the same as the two principal heads of civil jurisdiction: proceedings against morals offenders and disputes involving breach of promise.

It also appears that cases coming before the courts were decided by the same sorts of individuals who would have decided them if they had come before some local Congregational church. As has been noted, eighteenth-century Massachusetts rules of civil procedure gave juries broad discretion to decide both the law and the facts in the cases before them. Although they might take advice from a judge learned in the common law of England just as a congregation might take advice from a minister learned in the law of God,[125] juries, like the members of a congregation, were the ultimate law finders in every case that came before them. Moreover, juries were composed almost exclusively of men who attended the Congregational church. As discussed earlier, less than 3 percent of all jurors can be identified as having at any time in their lives joined a dissenting congregation. In short, there was a basic similarity between lay and ecclesiastical tribunals: men who served as jurors often performed a like function as members of their local Congregational meeting. The main difference between a congregation and a jury was that the former came from a single parish; juries, on the other hand, were drawn from all towns in the county by an essentially random process.

There is also reason to believe that juries and congregations both decided disputes in accordance with similar normative standards. Because records of jury deliberations have not been preserved, the normative standards that juries adopted cannot be known precisely. But some things seem clear. One is that the individuals who were assembled from different towns to form juries did not come together with radically different moral or ethical ideas, at least in reference to the sorts of disputes likely to come before them. Examination of the records of church adjudications of disputes in the various towns of eighteenth-century Plymouth reveals a striking similarity in the standards to which different congregations took recourse in resolving the cases before them. Because it appears from church records that moral norms among the different Congregational churches of eighteenth-century Plymouth were similar, it is likely that the members of those churches who came together to serve on juries also shared similar norms. Other direct evidence indicates that disputes were decided by the same standards whether they were decided in the church or the state. Norms that would today be associated with the secular courts were also used to help resolve disputes in the church, and norms that in the modern era would be identified as religious were simultaneously employed by the courts.

Thus, in one ecclesiastical case in Rochester, the complainants in a style reminiscent of common-law pleading of fictions charged the defendant with approaching a stack of hay belonging to them and attempting "violently that is contrary to our leave & against our wills to carry a load of it away."[126] Similarly, in the courts, jurors were being urged to use law to create "a Civil and Christian state"[127] where "all vice prophaneness & Immorality may be Suppressed & man-kind Reformed and Brought to act with a Due Regard to God,"[128] or being urged to bar collection of a debt in accordance with "the law of Moses [that] Interest for money lent to any of the Nation of the Jews is not allowable."[129] As a matter of common sense, of course, individuals who both went to church and served on juries and who had not yet completely partitioned their lives into distinct secular and religious spheres would be expected to apply the unitary set of norms with which they were familiar when asked to perform the same task—that of resolving disputes—whether the forum in which they were acting was church or court.

Yet, despite the obvious similarities between dispute-resolution proceedings in the churches and the courts, major differences also were evident. One was the more informal character of much ecclesiastical adjudication. Although procedures varied somewhat from church to church, it appears that individuals were usually encouraged to resolve their disputes before bringing them to the congregation. Thus, a person who felt aggrieved by another's unchristian conduct was normally required to seek redress from the alleged wrongdoer, if necessary with the assistance of the minister or some other leader of the church, before making a formal accusation before the entire church.[130] The First Church of Rochester, for example, directed potential claimants to "follow the Rule in 18 Mat 15:16 &c."—that is, first to confront the alleged wrongdoer individually, then to do so in the presence of witnesses, and only thereafter to appeal to the church. The parish indicated that it would "stand ready to hear" complaints only "if the first and secon[d] steps fail[ed]."[131] The church in Mattapoisett likewise enacted a rule providing that "No Matter of Difference between Brother, and Brother, shall be brought before the Chh, unless the two steps directed to, in the 18 of Matthew, be first taken."[132] Further evidence that many disputes were handled informally and brought officially before the church only after informal efforts had failed comes from a resolution of the church in Plymouth that, "if any Person in relation to this Chh shall be guilty of any Scandalous Offence," he would be proceeded against only if he did not first "within six months from the time of . . . [his] offence make . . . [his] Peace with the Chh,"[133] as well as from statements such as one in the Halifax records noting that "the Church were called together" to consider an "affair" only "after many private unsuccessful Endeavours for a Reconciliation."[134]

Once attempts to obtain informal redress had failed, formal proceedings were begun either by written complaint or oral accusation before the entire congregation during a Communion service. Some of the churches, like the First Church of Rochester, enacted formal procedural rules providing that "if any of the Brethren have any complaint to exhibit to the chh or which requires a church hearing, . . . they give it to the pastor in writing signed by them."[135] This rule, however, did not always insure that complaints came before the church in writing, for on at least one occasion, in Rochester—namely, "after Lecture 7 May 1756 Major Edward Winslow & Mr. Edward Morss applyed to the Brethren for advice with Relation to a difference between them."[136] In other churches, oral presentation of grievances was encouraged. In Wareham, it was voted unanimously that a church member could even "intercept yr communion . . . if anything shall arise in the carriage of any of the brethren that is an offense . . . to any that they have not time or opportunity to have ye matter heard before the Chh. before the communion."[137] Alternatively, an individual could simply decline to receive Communion and, when asked by the church to explain his refusal, report the alleged conduct of the member who had offended him.[138] Finally, a special procedure existed for bringing disputes between members and prospective members to the attention of the congregation: when an individual applied for membership in the church, existing members could object to admission on the basis of alleged wrongs committed by the applicant.[139]

Still another difference between the churches and the courts was the failure of the former to distinguish between criminal and noncriminal cases. This may be traced to a more fundamental difference between church and lay tribunals. Whereas modern courts, in particular, often conceive of the function of civil cases as at least partly compensatory and that of criminal cases as partly retributive, compensation and retribution were not the primary objectives of eighteenth-century ecclesiastical adjudication. The goal of the church was to encourage disputants "to lay aside Contention . . . and to forgive one another for Cxt [Christ's] sake."[140] The church sought to induce people "to come to a mutual Agreemt respecting their old Difference" and to make "their Interchangible acknowlegmts of their Faults one to another & therein mutually agree . . . to bury all the sd former Difference in oblivion."[141] Indeed, in Titicut, a temporary settlement of communal divisions resulted in "mutual rejoicing together" and "a Remarkable Solemn Season with us" during which the church "had a glorious Sacrament together."[142] In short, the churches sought to insure that any "Difficulty subsisting between" individuals would be "accommodated"[143] "for peace sake."[144] Like towns, churches would strive for peace and harmony by voting "to Suspend determining anything" in cases where they did not have "sufficient light to act" and by "waiting for more clearness" before acting.[145] Like towns, churches sometimes "talked over Sundry things but nothing voted,"[146] and like towns and juries, they recognized the relationship between harmony and voting "unanimously."[147]

People had rather clear visions of what constituted orderly and disorderly church communities. A community was disorderly when a church suffered from "unhappy Divisions" as a result of having members "of a Controverting Disposition"[148] or "the Chh [otherwise] seemed to be too much in Parties."[149] Accordingly, it was appropriate for the church "to look into somethings in . . . [the] Conduct" of individuals which "had occasioned uneasiness among some of the Brethren,"[150] for such uneasiness could lead to greater discord. Nor was it uncommon for an individual to confess his sense of guilt if there was "a Division in ye chh . . . upon my account"[151] or if "sundry Uncomfortable differences [arose] between my Neighbrs & mys to ye grief of good Christians."[152] Indeed, church members could be suspended from Communion if they acted in ways that "tended to Divide the Body of Christ."[153] In an orderly community, on the other hand, individuals would not engage in continual disputation but would instead show "charity" toward each other[154] and would "be carefull of Doing any thing unto our Neighbors from a spirit of Revenge."[155]

The determination to achieve order through harmony is reflected in church proceedings. Congregations dealt harshly with any individual who "refused . . . Satesfaction to the Church"[156] or otherwise "behaved himself very obstinately & turbulently."[157] This was true in the case of a Middleboro man who, though he was willing to confess his substantive offense, refused to join with it an "acknowledgement of his repeated Contempt of ye Chh—nor of his falsehoods Under this process."[158] Accordingly, he was permitted to rot in debtor's prison without receiving any aid from the church. Likewise, in Titicut, the church set aside a special "day of fasting & prayer" when one woman failed "to ackneledge her Sin nor so much as manifest a desire of returning to God & this people."[159] When the woman persisted in her refusal to acknowledge the church's authority, she was excommunicated.[160]

For a confession to be fully satisfactory, it was not only necessary for persons in conflict to confess to the church, it was also necessary for "ye Parties in Contention" to give "Christian Satisfaction &c."—that is, to confess to each other.[161] If an individual refused to make proper "Confessions to these offended Brethren"[162] or if he offered "a Confession . . . which . . . the offended" with good reason "would not accept,"[163] the guilty individual would not be received back into the fold of the church. The principal objective of a church adjudication was simply that all disputants make peace with each other, not that fault be adjudicated or that retribution or compensation necessarily be obtained. This fact can emerge no more clearly than from a Wareham case, where, after the church had looked upon all the "evidences however true," it simply decided to leave the dispute unresolved, thinking "it proper for peace sake to bury all." Therefore, the church resolved that the defendant's evidence was "satisfactory to clear him from ye charge laid in against him . . . & yt he ought be restored to our charity" and that the plaintiff should also be "looked upon as clear from ye scandal of asserting a falsehood to ye Chh. & so was now [also] in full charity . . . upon ye account."[164]

A final difference between dispute-resolution proceedings in Congregational churches and analogous proceedings in the courts was the nature of the sanctions. Courts proceeded, of course, by ordering the seizure of property or the arrest of a defendant. On the other hand, the only sanctions that a church could normally impose were censure, public confession, repentance, and restitution, backed up by the ultimate sanction of excommunication.[165] As a result of the nature of these sanctions and the structure of the Congregationalist religious order, the jurisdiction of the church was limited. Ecclesiastical discipline was effective only against the members of each individual congregation. The core difficulty was that each congregation was a separate and independent entity that was linked formally to other congregations only by councils of delegates drawn from neighboring churches that were expensive and cumbersome to convene;[166] individual congregations neither heard claims presented by members of another congregation nor imposed sanctions upon them.[167]

It must be stressed, however, that in many parishes nearly everyone who resided in the community was probably a member of the church, though there were two classes of membership. On the one hand, the concept of membership was a narrow one for the purposes of determining who could hear and adjudicate a dispute; only full communicants, who had made a full profession of faith, were permitted to participate as members of the congregational body that decided the case.

On the other hand, the definition of membership often was broad for purposes of discipline, subjecting anyone who had been baptised, even if only on the strength of some distant ancestor's full profession of faith, to ecclesiastical sanctions.[168] A clear example of the church's disciplinary power over nonmembers who had nonetheless been baptized comes from Halifax, where Jonathan Drew, Jr., was denied admission to full communion and sent "a letter of Admonition" because "he is under our watch & Care as a Baptized Person, and . . . Still persists in his Impenitence."[169] The result, of course, was that any baptized resident of a community who would feel the sting of a censure by its moral leaders was subject to the discipline of the church, while all who lived outside the community were not.

Because the church had no effective jurisdiction over disputes between members of different congregations, those cases had to be taken to court if they could not be resolved informally. On the other hand, the power of the local congregation over its own members was great. It was a power reinforced perhaps by inherited traditions that many had accepted in the seventeenth century—traditions that encouraged church members to settle disputes without recourse to the courts.[170] It was a power that made many local congregations into viable dispute-resolution institutions within their own parishes.

Thus, two forums were available for the resolution of most intracommunity disputes other than those disputes of a political nature that were heard in town meeting. The question that arises is why disputants would select one forum in preference to the other. Most of the differences between the two were likely irrelevant to most litigants. But several differences were significant. One tended to favor taking disputes to court; the others to favor going to the church. The advantage of the courts lay in the power of the sheriff to arrest people and attach goods, a power that enabled the courts to reach individuals in a town who were not amenable to moral suasion by the church. One advantage of the church lay in the informality of its proceedings. Another was that the local church met regularly and close to home, whereas the Inferior Court of Common Pleas met only four times per year at the county seat, which was distant from the homes of most litigants. Going to court also typically involved the expense of hiring a lawyer. As will appear in the next chapter, these practical advantages seem to have made the church the predominant institution in most pre-Revolutionary communities for the resolution of disputes between members, with the courts serving only in a back-up capacity.

3 Judicial Resolution of Disputes between Members of the Same Community, 1725–1774

It is possible to move, at least in part, beyond impressionistic description of procedures used by the towns, courts, and churches in eighteenth-century Plymouth and of the sorts of conflicts and disputes they heard. This and the following two chapters will present a statistical analysis of a significant aspect of eighteenth-century dispute resolution—namely, litigation in the courts. Unfortunately, the entire dispute-resolution process cannot be subjected to such analysis because the town and church records are often incomplete and thus fail to provide a reliable sample upon which to base conclusions. Court records, however, are sufficiently complete to permit careful analysis of litigation patterns. Analysis of litigation will, in turn, offer indirect insight into the process of dispute resolution in the church.

To the extent that each local church was functioning effectively to resolve disputes between members of the community in which the church was located, the practical advantages of the church would lead one to expect that few cases involving only members of that community would come to court and hence that most litigation in the courts would involve parties from different communities. In fact, during the half-century between 1725 and 1774, 70 percent[1] of all cases between residents of Plymouth County that came before the Inferior Court of Common Pleas, the court having original jurisdiction over all actions other than small claims in which the crown was not a party, involved litigants who resided in different communities; only 2,537 out of a total of 8,360 cases involved parties who resided in the same community.[2] These 2,537 cases, moreover, were not evenly distributed among the fourteen towns in the county. More than two-thirds of the intracommunity cases—a total of 1,789 cases in all[3]—arose in five of the towns, containing only 39 percent of the county's population,[4] while the remaining 748 cases[5] arose in the other nine towns. In one group of towns, neighbors took each other to court far less frequently than they did in the other group. This chapter will compare intracommunity litigation patterns in these two groups of towns in an effort to isolate differences in the nature of litigation that may assist in explaining the differences in its quantity. This exercise in comparative analysis must begin by presenting some basic data on the nonlitigious group of towns, initially in noncomparative form.

The Nine Nonlitigious Towns

Before turning to intracommunity litigation data on the nine nonlitigious towns, which were Abington, Bridgewater, Duxbury, Halifax, Kingston, Marshfield, Middleboro, Plympton, and Wareham, it is necessary to define the meaning for our purposes of the term "community." Because of the importance of the church in nonjudicial processes of dispute resolution, I normally understand an eighteenth-century Plymouth County community to consist of those people who attended the same local church; inasmuch as provincial law in general required all residents of a territorial parish to attend the Congregational church in that parish,[6] most communities were bounded geographically by parish lines.

Five of the nonlitigious towns—Abington, Duxbury, Halifax, Kingston, and Wareham—each contained one parish, and its boundaries were identical to the boundaries of the town. Hence, when reference is made to intracommunity litigation in these towns, the discussion concerns cases in which all parties resided in the same town. The other four towns, however, contained more than one parish.

Bridgewater, for example, contained four entire parishes—North, South, East, and West—plus part of the Titicut Parish, the other part of which lay in Middleboro. Accordingly, reference to an intracommunity case in Bridgewater designates a case in which all litigants lived in a single parish.[7] Because judicial records list only the town and not the parish in which litigants resided, it has been necessary to make a statistical estimate of the amount of intratown litigation in Bridgewater that was of an intracommunity nature. The process of making this estimate was complicated by the loss of parish records in two of the five parishes in Bridgewater.[8] This made it necessary to determine the residence of litigants by means other than recourse to parish lists. The method chosen was to compile lists of people buried in the town's cemeteries, on the theory that place of burial, at least in eighteenth-century agrarian Massachusetts, where travel was somewhat difficult, would usually reflect a deceased's place of residence before his death. By examining cemetery lists for East, West, and South Bridgewater published by Williams Latham[9] and by compiling lists from gravestones for two cemeteries in Titicut[10] and seven in North Bridgewater,[11] it was possible to generate information on the probable residence of all litigants in 58 cases—approximately 15 percent of all intratown cases in Bridgewater. In 37 cases, or 64 percent of the total,[12] the litigation involved residents of two or more parishes, while in 21 cases, or 36 percent of the total, all litigants resided in the same parish.

This 15-percent sample poses two difficulties. One is that, because of the small size of the intraparish sample—21 cases spread over five parishes—and the impossibility of generating any other accurate data, including population data, for the individual parishes, it is possible to analyze intraparish litigation in Bridgewater only as a unit, which consists of 36 percent of the intratown litigation. The other difficulty is that, although the 15-percent sample is in most respects random, there is one way in which it is not: it does not include transients who moved out of town before they died. If it were assumed that transients had weaker ties to their communities than nontransients and hence were more likely to take part in litigation with their neighbors, then failure to include them in the sample would result in underestimation of the total number of intracommunity cases. I am convinced, however, that this possible underestimation does not vitiate the findings delineated in this book. Many people who moved out of communities undoubtedly left for personal reasons having nothing to do with their relationship to their neighbors, such as a desire to marry a partner in another town, a desire to live near relatives, an opportunity to acquire a larger and better tract of land in a new locality, or some other chance for economic advancement. Many other transients surely had strong communal roots.[13]

But, in any event, the difficulty of identifying the transient population makes it impossible in the context of this study to explore systematically the impact of transients upon the cohesiveness of New England communities. It may be that those having a large population of unrooted transients had much more litigation than communities having few such transients. It may also be that the exclusion of transients from the samples used for determining the quantity of intracommunity litigation results in some underestimation of the absolute quantity of Bridgewater litigation, though not a serious underestimation when the data for Bridgewater is examined comparatively against data from other towns and other time periods.[14] In the end, the definition of intracommunity litigation in Bridgewater—36 percent of the town's intratown litigation—should be understood as a necessarily imperfect but usable measure that has been extrapolated from the 58-case cemetery sample.

Middleboro was similar to Bridgewater in that it contained two entire parishes—Center and Lake—as well as the portion of Titicut Parish not contained in Bridgewater. Thus, the same techniques that were used to estimate Bridgewater's quantity of intracommunity litigation were used to estimate Middleboro's. In addition, a further complication arose from the fact that, whereas Bridgewater's five parishes were of approximately equal size, Middleboro's were not. The Center Parish comprised about two-thirds of the town and stretched from Bridgewater and Taunton, in the north and west, to Wareham, in the southeast—a distance of some twelve miles. The Center Parish was divided, moreover, into several apparently distinct villages. The oldest was the town center, located on the main east-west highway from Plymouth to Taunton and Providence, Rhode Island, where that highway intersected with the southwestern highway to Dartmouth and Newport. The Center Parish church was located at the town center. Some four miles to the northwest was the small settlement of the Warren family known today as Warrenton. About an equal distance to the northeast was the Eddy family settlement known today as Eddyville. Five miles southeast of the town center was a small settlement now called Rock Village, where a Baptist church was founded in 1763, and three miles farther to the southeast there was yet another settlement. But the most important separate group of settlements grew up beginning in the 1730s a mere two miles west of the town center at a series of power sites along the Nemasket River. Apparently a continuous rivalry existed between the inhabitants of the new river settlements and those of the old town center, initially sparked by opposition of much of the town to the construction of the first milldam on the river.[15] This rivalry was probably exacerbated in the 1740s, when a schism in the Center Parish church,[16] which may have been related to the appearance of these new settlements, coincided with a sharp rise in Middleboro's intratown litigation rate.[17] The rivalry continued into the nineteenth century, when one of the river settlements, Four Corners Village, grew into the present Middleboro Center while the old town center declined to nothing more than the parish church and its accompanying cemetery.[18]

Because of the size of the Center Parish, which was simply too large geographically to be an intimate community, and the enduring rivalry between the old town center and the river settlements, I have concluded that Middleboro contained four separate communities: Lake Parish, Titicut Parish, the river settlements, and that part of the Center Parish located east of the river settlements. By examining published lists of burials in the cemeteries at the river settlements and the old town center[19] and by compiling lists for fourteen other cemeteries in the town,[20] it was possible to identify all the litigants in 73 intratown cases—almost an exact one-in-six sample.[21] In 63 percent of the sample cases, the litigants came from more than one of the separate communities identified above, while in 37 percent all the litigants were members of the same compact settlement. For reasons that have already been given above in discussing Bridgewater, this 37-percent figure will be used to delimit in a necessarily approximate but still useful way the total amount of intracommunity litigation in Middleboro.

The final two towns, Marshfield, and Plympton, also contained more than one parish. In the case of Plympton, there were two parishes: North and South. In 1790, the latter was incorporated into the town of Carver.[22] By examining published records for two cemeteries in the North Parish[23] and compiling lists for four cemeteries in the South Parish,[24] it was possible to generate a sample of 24 cases. In 21 of them, or 88 percent of the total,[25] the litigation was of an intracommunity nature in that all of the litigants were residents of the same parish. However, in Marshfield, which also contained two parishes,[26] it was possible because of the small number of intratown cases to generate a sample of only 15 cases in which the parish of all litigants could be identified—clearly too small a sample to be statistically useful.[27] Thus, in Marshfield intracommunity litigation is assumed to be the same as intratown litigation—a definition that somewhat overestimates the intracommunity total.[28]

Given these definitions of intracommunity litigation, table 3.1 lists the number of intracommunity cases in each of the nonlitigious towns for the entire period, 1725–74; the average number of cases per year; and the average per year per 1,000 inhabitants.[29] As table 3.1 shows, the amount of intracommunity litigation in most towns tended to be between 1 and 2 cases per 1,000 residents per year. Standing in isolation, this number is, of course, quite meaningless; there is no way to know whether one or two intracommunity cases per year was a large or a small amount of litigation. It will appear, however, as the analysis progresses, that the difference among the litigation rates of the nine towns is small compared with the difference between the rates for the nine towns and the rates for the towns in which litigation was high.

TABLE 3.1 Nine Nonlitigious Towns: Intracommunity Cases, 1725–1774[30]

	Total Cases	*Cases per Year*	*Cases per Year per 1,000 Inhabitants*
Abington	44	0.88	0.70
Bridgewater[31]	146	2.92	0.74
Duxbury	135	2.70	2.57
Halifax	9	0.22	0.40
Kingston	75	1.53	2.02
Marshfield	61	1.22	1.06
Middleboro[32]	162	3.24	0.95
Plympton[33]	104	2.08	1.50
Wareham	12	0.33	0.66

The low rate of litigation in the nine towns can also be expressed by examining the percentage of total population that appeared in court.[34] The difficulty of obtaining information about the community in which each litigant resided precludes analysis of this percentage at the intracommunity level. Instead, it is necessary to examine intratown litigation. Table 3.2 lists for each of the nine towns the percentage of its population appearing in an intratown case on 1 or 2 occasions in their lives, between 3 and 7 occasions, and on 8 or more occasions;[35] the final column of the table adds the first three in order to state the percentage of each town's population that ever appeared in court. Because the data presented in this table is for intratown rather than intracommunity litigation, one problem presented by the data in table 3.1—namely, that litigation in Bridgewater, Middleboro, and Plympton may have been underestimated—is not present here. As table 3.2 shows, less than 10 percent of the population of seven of the

TABLE 3.2 Nine Nonlitigious Towns: Percentage of Population Appearing in Intratown Cases, 1725–1774

	One or Two Times	*Three–Seven Times*	*Eight or More Times*	*At Any Time*
Abington	4.3%	0.6%	0.0%	4.9%
Bridgewater	6.8%	2.1%	0.4%	9.3%
Duxbury	10.4%	3.0%	0.5%	13.9%
Halifax	2.5%	0.2%	0.0%	2.7%
Kingston	5.9%	2.3%	0.5%	8.7%
Marshfield	7.1%	1.0%	0.0%	8.1%
Middleboro	8.4%	2.1%	0.7%	11.2%
Plympton	7.1%	2.2%	0.1%	9.4%
Wareham	3.8%	0.4%	0.0%	4.2%

nine towns ever appeared in an intratown case, and in the two remaining towns, Duxbury and Middleboro, the percentages of the populations appearing in at least one such case were 14 and 11 percent, respectively. Moreover, very few individuals in any of the nine towns were highly litigious, a category here defined as the appearance in an intratown case on 8 or more occasions in a lifetime. In fact, in no town was as much as 1 percent of the population highly litigious.

Taken as a unit, the nine towns produced only forty-nine men during the entire half century between 1725 and 1774 who appeared in 8 or more intratown cases in their lifetimes. When they are examined as a group, it appears that few of the forty-nine were among the elite leaders of their respective towns. On the contrary, many of them were troublemakers who appear not to have been responsive to community social control, while a few were former members of the elite who had either withdrawn or been cast out of it.

One such litigious outcast was Thomas Palmer of Middleboro, who had served as the minister of the Center church until 1708, when he was "removed from the work of the Gospel ministry, and suspended from communion at the Lord's table for his scandalous immoralities"[36]—namely, his drunkenness. He then became the town physician, a profession that did not have the high status in the eighteenth century that it has today, and was not restored to Communion until he confessed his sins in 1737, six years before his death.[37]

Equally troublesome was Joshua Soul, of Duxbury. He must have been descended from a family of some status because he was chosen by the town to perform a number of important tasks as a relatively young man. In 1728, for example, he was elected moderator of the town meeting, and in 1735 he was chosen as one of three agents to procure a schoolmaster. He again served as such an agent in 1736. But his most important appointment came in 1737, when he was appointed one of five agents to "treat with" the local minister "about the matter relating to his salary, which hath been lately controverted at Court." Up to the time of this appointment, Soul himself had never been a litigant in court. Apparently, the minister and the agents reached an agreement that the town meeting then rejected, leaving Soul unhappy and inducing him, along with several other residents, to "enter their protest against the said town's proceeding any further in their contention with . . . [the minister] in the law about his salary."

The next year, 1738, Soul brought his first lawsuit, which was followed by two additional ones during the next decade, a period during which Soul's name is conspicuously absent from the town meeting records. Soul next appears in Duxbury records in 1748 and subsequent years as an agent performing minor tasks for the proprietors of the common, undivided lands in Duxbury and Pembroke. Then, in 1750, he was appointed agent of the proprietors "to sue the said town of Duxborough or any of the inhabitants thereof" so as to protect the proprietors' rights against townsmen who did not own shares in the common lands. During the next four years, he was a party in at least five separate suits, including one against the proprietors for his wages. For reasons that are unknown, the town voted to pay the judgment Soul obtained against the proprietors and sent three agents to visit him "and haunt him, and use persuasive arguments with him for to abate some part of his execution" against the proprietors.[38] The records thereafter are silent, and it may well be that some compromise was reached and that Soul was thereafter sufficiently reintegrated into the life of the community so as not to take his disputes to court, for his name never appeared again as a litigant until 1772, when the administrator of his estate brought a suit in his name. What is clear is that, during the time he was an active litigant, Soul did not actively participate in community life except as an adversary of the town in his capacity as agent for the proprietors.

Another frequent litigant was Ebenezer Morton, of Middleboro, who lived in Four Corners Village and whose wife, "a devout christian woman . . . of strong will and energy, became a leader of the sect called the 'New Lights.'"[39] Although Morton served four terms in the key post of selectman, all his service occurred from 1744 to 1747, at the height of the schism in the Center church between the New and Old Lights, perhaps in recognition of the need to give all parties in an increasingly divided town representation on the town board; once the schism was healed, his leadership role ceased.[40]

Thirteen other men who appeared in civil cases 8 or more times in their lives evidenced their lack of amenability to community controls by the fact that they were also indicted on criminal charges in the Superior Court and Court of General

Sessions of the Peace. One of these men, Benanuel Leach of Bridgewater, was the county's most prosecuted thief; the apparent organizer of a sheep-stealing ring that operated in Bridgewater and in neighboring towns, he was indicted on nine separate charges. Of the remaining twelve frequent litigants who also appeared in court on criminal charges, three were indicted on two separate charges, two were indicted on three charges, and one each was indicted on four, five, and six charges, respectively. Four each were indicted once.

Apart from those who have already been discussed, only nine out of the forty-nine highly litigious men held important church or town offices, such as deacon, selectman, town treasurer, town meeting moderator, or representative to the General Court.[41] Two of these nine probably preferred to have their disputes adjudicated by judicial rather than community institutions. One was Nicholas Sever, of Kingston, who served as a selectman and moderator of the town meeting and sat on several important committees. But his principal office lay outside the town. For twenty-five years, he was a judge of the county's Inferior Court of Common Pleas. A prominent appointee of the royal governor in Boston, he was by virtue of his office an advocate of legal rather than communitarian resolution of disputes. Hence, it is not surprising that he brought the controversies in which he was involved to court.

The same was probably also true of Elkanah Leonard, of Middleboro, who served the town as selectman and as representative to the General Court. Leonard, however, was also a practicing lawyer—the second in the town—and a justice of the peace; like Sever, he was by virtue of his royal appointment and even more by virtue of his occupation an advocate of legal rather than communitarian resolution of disputes. Moreover, in the mid-1740s Leonard suffered some sort of mental breakdown that impaired his stability during the remaining thirty years of his life, the period during which he made the majority of his appearances in court as a litigant.[42]

Only five additional men out of the forty-nine highly litigious ones can be identified as having held lesser town offices, such as constable, Sabbath warden, militia captain, or town committee post. On the basis of an examination of town histories and town records, it appears that approximately thirty out of forty-nine were never chosen to any town or church office at all in a society where low-level officeholding was quite widespread.[43] In other words, while a few of the forty-nine most litigious men in the nine towns were among their town's elite, the group of forty-nine as a whole was not especially distinguished and, indeed, contained more outcasts and troublemakers than it did town leaders.

When cases in which these forty-nine litigious individuals appeared are subtracted from the total number of intratown cases in each of the nine towns, rather few remain. Table 3.3 lists for each town the total number of intratown cases involving only residents who appeared in court in seven or fewer cases during their lives; it also gives the average number of such cases per year per 1,000 residents. Because table 3.3 is derived from an intratown rather than an intracommunity case sample, there is, again, no problem of underinclusive estimates. As table 3.3 shows, nonlitigious residents accounted for an average of between one and two intratown cases per thousand residents per year in most towns. In short, an examination of litigation statistics for the nine nonlitigious towns generally indicates that, once cases involving a small number of highly litigious individuals are removed from the total sample, there was very little litigation among fellow townsmen—slightly more than one case per year per thousand residents. Moreover, as table 3.2 suggests, only about one-tenth of each

TABLE 3.3 Nine Nonlitigious Towns: Intratown Cases Not Involving Highly Litigious Residents, 1725–1774

	Total Cases	*Cases per Year per 1,000 Residents*
Abington	44	0.70
Bridgewater	244	1.24
Duxbury	98	1.87
Halifax	9	0.40
Kingston	40	1.08
Marshfield	61	1.06
Middleboro	201	1.18
Plympton	108	1.55
Wareham	12	0.66

town's population ever participated in this litigation. The statistical analysis will now be further refined by examining data for the nine nonlitigious towns in comparison with data from five other more litigious towns.

Hanover and Pembroke: The Quaker Towns

In 1707, a Quaker meetinghouse was built on the boundary line between the two small and otherwise typically nonlitigious towns of Pembroke and Hanover.[44] This had a profound effect on litigation patterns because the Congregational churches in the two towns proved unable to resolve disputes between their own members and the Friends; many such disputes had to be turned over to the courts. In a meaningful sense, Congregationalists and Quakers who were neighbors, precisely because they did not partake of the same Communion, were not truly members of the same community. But not only does one find litigation in the two towns between Congregationalists and Quakers; one also finds cases in which all the parties had joined the Society of Friends.[45] The apparent explanation is that the Pembroke Monthly Meeting, unlike some other Quaker meetings, gave its members permission to take each other to court. Although this meeting dealt with a number of disputes between its members, including a case brought for nonpayment of a debt[46] and a case brought to obtain a settlement of accounts,[47] it also resolved that a "friend as the case may be may sue a friend and not be accounted to brake the good order Established amongst friends."[48]

Quakers, who probably constituted about 10 percent of the population of Hanover and Pembroke,[49] accounted for the largest portion of the litigation within the two towns during the 1720s and 1730s. Between 1725 and 1739, they appeared on at least one side in 102 of Pembroke's 149 intratown cases, or 68 percent of the total. Over the same period, they appeared in 32 of Hanover's 75 intratown cases, or 43 percent of the total. As a result of the presence of litigation involving Quakers during those fifteen years, Pembroke averaged 9.93 cases per year. This is an unusually high figure compared, for example, to the Duxbury figure of 2.70 per year, the highest among the nine nonlitigious towns. Similarly, Hanover had an average of 5.00 cases per year, also a somewhat high figure. When the Quaker cases are subtracted from the totals, however, Pembroke's total number of cases for the fifteen years falls to 47, an average of 3.13 per year, and Hanover's total falls to 43, an average of 2.87 per year.[50] These latter numbers are within the range reported in table 3.1 as typical for most communities in the county.

Beginning in 1740, litigation rates in both Pembroke and Hanover began to decline. Between 1740 and 1774, there was a total of 161 cases in Pembroke, an average of 4.60 instead of 9.93 cases per year. During the same period in Hanover, there were 93 cases in all, an average of 2.66 instead of 5.00 cases per year. Nearly all this decline is attributable to a drop in cases in which Quakers appeared as parties. After 1740, Quakers, who had previously accounted for 68 percent of Pembroke's litigation, accounted for only 30 percent, appearing in only 49 of the 161 cases. This left 112 cases in which they did not appear, an average of 3.20 cases per year that was almost identical to the pre-1740 non-Quaker average of 3.13 cases per year. In Hanover, Quakers after 1740 accounted for only 23 percent of all the cases, appearing in a total of 21 of them. This left 72 cases, or an average of 2.06 per year in which they did not appear. This average is somewhat lower than the pre-1740 non-Quaker average of 2.87 per year.

It is not surprising that litigation involving Quakers, especially litigation between Quakers and Congregationalists, should have declined after 1740.[51] Two developments around that time eased tensions between the two religious groups and thereby facilitated the integration of Quakers into Massachusetts communities. One was the passage between 1728 and 1737 of legislation that exempted Quakers from the payment of taxes for the support of the Congregational religious establishment.[52] As a result of this legislation, Quakers were less perceived and perceived themselves less as enemies of the Congregationalist religious order. The other event was the Great Awakening. Beginning in 1740, it spawned a variety of radical religious movements that made Quakers by comparison seem tame, conservative, and scarcely a threat to the standing order. Although Quakers, of course, never became a part of the Congregational religious order, they ceased to threaten dismantlement of the order. After 1740, the more serious threats to the Congregationalist establishment came from newer groups such as the Baptists. All of these factors encouraged the acceptance of Quakers in their local communities, and, although churches still remained unable to adjudicate disputes between Congregationalists and Quakers, other less formal channels between the two groups may have arisen for that purpose.

Overall, it is clear that the religious division between Congregationalists and Quakers in Pembroke and Hanover accounted for the unusual amount of litigation in those towns.[53] When cases involving at least one Quaker are subtracted from Pembroke's total of 310 cases between 1725 and 1774, only 159, or 3.18 cases per year, remain. When adjusted for population, the Pembroke figure works out to 2.26 non-Quaker cases per 1,000 residents per year, an amount below the Duxbury average of 2.57, which was the highest average among the nine nonlitigious towns. Similarly, when 53 Quaker cases are subtracted from Hanover's total of 168, 115 cases, or an average of 2.30 per year, is left. When further adjusted for population, the Hanover average is 2.12 non-Quaker cases per 1,000 inhabitants per year.

As was true in the nine nonlitigious towns, a few individuals accounted for a substantial portion of the intratown litigation occurring in Hanover and Pembroke. In Pembroke, 213 separate litigants made a total of 653 appearances in the town's 310 cases. Sixteen of these litigants, who each appeared on 8 or more occasions, accounted for 293 appearances, or 45 percent of the total. The 16 appeared in 212 of the 310 cases, leaving only 98 cases, or 1.96 per year, in which the rest of the residents of the town sued each other. Only 44 other people living in Pembroke during the half century between 1725 and 1774 appeared in litigation more than twice in their entire lives; they constituted a mere 3 percent of the 1765 population. Another 153 individuals, or 11 percent of the 1765 population, appeared once or twice in court against another town resident.

Similarly, in Hanover, only 116 different residents came to court in its 168 cases, making a total of 367 appearances. Eleven out of the 116, who each appeared 8 or more times, accounted for 148 appearances, or 40 percent of the 367 total. The 11 appeared in 97 cases, leaving only 71 cases, or 1.42 per year, in which the remaining town residents sued each other. Only 29 other residents of Hanover, or 3 percent of the 1765 population, ever appeared more than twice in intratown litigation, and only 76, or 7 percent of the population, ever appeared either once or twice. Although Pembroke, in particular, had a higher percentage of its population involved in litigation than any of the nine nonlitigious towns—15 percent in all—this figure was not far above the range reported in table 3.2 for the nine towns, while the corresponding Hanover figure of 11 percent was within that range.

As was also true in the other nine towns in the county, the residents of Hanover and Pembroke who were most litigious were not, on the whole, leaders of their towns. In Pembroke, for example, eight of the sixteen most litigious residents were Quakers, and three of the remaining eight litigants appeared in criminal as well as civil court: John Keen and Isaac Soul on one occasion each and John Russell on two. Three other litigants have left no records by which their position in town life can be identified. This leaves only two men who can be identified as town leaders: Isaac Little and Josiah Keen, both of whom were justices of the peace who also served the town as representatives to the General Court.[54] The pattern for Hanover is not sharply different, though data is somewhat thinner. There, six of the eleven most litigious residents have left no trace in local histories. Of the remaining five, one was a Quaker and two left their only trace in criminal records, one being indicted once and the other twice. The final two men, Joseph Stockbridge and Thomas Josselyn, were residents of some prominence. Both were deacons in the local Congregational church and both served the town as selectmen, and Josselyn also served as representative to the General Court.[55]

As was suggested at the outset of this section, the litigation patterns of Hanover and Pembroke did not differ significantly from the patterns of the nine nonlitigious towns, except in one respect. The sole important difference was that, especially during the 1720s and 1730s, Quakers, who were not well integrated into community life and hence were not able to use communitarian mechanisms for resolving disputes effectively, brought an unusually large number of intratown cases to court. In view of the importance of the Congregational church to communitarian dispute resolution, the extraordinary presence of Quaker litigants before the Inferior Court of Common Pleas is not at all surprising, for in eighteenth-century Massachusetts, one would expect religious dissent to interrupt normal patterns of communitarian dispute settlement and life.

Plymouth: The County's Commercial Capital

When intratown litigation statistics for the town of Plymouth are compared with those of the nine nonlitigious towns, even more striking differences emerge than in the case of Hanover and Pembroke. Between 1725 and 1774, the town of Plymouth, the county seat and commercial capital of the region, had a total of 891 cases in which residents of the town sued each other, or 17.82 cases per year. Thus, Plymouth, the fourth largest town in the county with about half the population of Bridgewater and substantially fewer inhabitants than Middleboro, experienced more than twice as much litigation as either of those towns. Indeed, Plymouth had more than six times as many cases as Duxbury, though it had only about twice as many inhabitants. What accounts for this extreme litigiousness?

Unlike Bridgewater and Middleboro, the political entity known as the town of Plymouth did not consist of a number of smaller, distinct communities. Although Kingston and Plympton had once been part of the town, they had become fully separate by the 1720s. Thereafter, the only community that existed separate from the town center was the small settlement of Manomet Beach. Although a parish was organized there in 1731 and a church with twenty-five members was gathered in 1747,[56] Manomet was then as today a tiny village of less than two hundred people.[57] Unfortunately, Manomet was too small to permit, by way of the sampling procedures used in Bridgewater and Middleboro, reliable determination of the percentage of Plymouth litigation in which Manomet residents appeared.[58] It seems unlikely, however, that this small village accounted for very much of Plymouth's litigation, and hence Plymouth's intratown litigation is treated as all intracommunity.

What differentiated litigation in Plymouth was the commercial character of the litigants. Seventy-seven percent of the intracommunity litigation before the Inferior Court of Common Pleas—683 of Plymouth's 891 cases—involved at least one litigant engaged in commerce, which is here defined as including trading, maritime activity, and the manufacture of products to be sold in markets outside the town. When these cases are subtracted from the total, only 208 noncommercial cases, or an average of 4.16 cases per year, remain. Bridgewater, in comparison, had 120 noncommercial, intracommunity cases between 1725 and 1774, or 2.40 per year, and Middleboro had 112 such cases, or 2.24 per year. Cases in which commercial litigants appeared seem, for reasons that will be discussed in the final chapter, to account for nearly all the disparity between Plymouth and the nonlitigious towns in the community. No other variable or group of variables and no other criteria for determining the commercial character of cases can account for even half as much of the variance between Plymouth and the nonlitigious towns.[59]

Table 3.4 presents data for each town, first with respect to the total number of intracommunity cases in the town in which none of the litigants was engaged in a trading, maritime, or industrial occupation, and second with respect to the average number of cases per year per 1,000 residents. As table 3.4 shows, Plymouth still manifested the second highest rate of litigation in the county even after cases involving com-

TABLE 3.4 Twelve Towns: Noncommercial Intracommunity Cases, 1725–1774

	Total Cases	*Cases per Year per 1,000 Residents*
Pembroke[60]	226	3.21
Plymouth	208	1.91
Hanover[60]	90	1.66
Duxbury	77	1.47
Plympton[61]	85	1.22
Kingston	34	0.91
Marshfield	38	0.66
Middleboro[62]	112	0.66
Bridgewater[63]	120	0.61
Abington	28	0.44
Wareham	8	0.44
Halifax	5	0.22

mercial parties are removed from the sample. However, the table also shows that Plymouth's litigation rate was not dramatically different from the rates of other towns, particularly when it is recalled that some part of its litigation embraced residents of Manomet.[64]

Given the large amount of intracommunity litigation that occurred in Plymouth, it is not surprising that Plymouth also differed from the nonlitigious towns in the county in that a much larger percentage of its population appeared in court. A total of 524 Plymouth residents appeared in 891 intratown cases on a total of 2,003 occasions. Sixty-six of those residents, who each appeared in 8 or more cases, accounted for 1,012 appearances, or 51 percent of the total of 2,003 appearances. Table 3.5, which states the percentages of the 1765 population of each town appearing in court either 1 or 2 times in their lives, between 3 and 7 times, 8 or more times, and at least 1 time, shows that Plymouth's residents appeared in court with unusual frequency in all the categories. It should be noted, however, that the nonlitigious inhabitants of Plymouth appeared in court with unusual frequency only in cases in which a litigious inhabitant was also a party. When cases involving the 66 townspeople who appeared in court on 8 or more occasions are subtracted from the Plymouth intratown total, only 171 cases remain, for an average of 1.57 cases per year per 1,000 residents. This average is little different from those for several of the nonlitigious towns given in table 3.3

Yet another significant difference between Plymouth and the other towns is in the nature of the residents who appeared frequently in the Court of Common Pleas. In all the other towns considered so far, the litigious inhabitants normally were not its leading citizens but those who hardly participated in community life. They were either troublemakers, individuals under effective ostracism, or people who, in many

TABLE 3.5 Twelve Towns: Percentage of Frequency of Appearances by Residents, 1725–1774

	One or Two Times	*Three–Seven Times*	*Eight or More Times*	*At Any Time*
Abington	4.3%	0.6%	0.0%	4.9%
Bridgewater	6.8%	2.1%	0.4%	9.3%
Duxbury	10.4%	3.0%	0.5%	13.9%
Halifax	2.5%	0.2%	0.0%	2.7%
Hanover	7.0%	2.7%	1.0%	10.7%
Kingston	5.9%	2.3%	0.5%	8.7%
Marshfield	7.1%	1.0%	0.0%	8.1%
Middleboro	8.4%	2.1%	0.7%	11.2%
Pembroke	10.9%	3.1%	1.1%	15.1%
Plymouth	14.8%	6.2%	3.0%	24.0%
Plympton	7.1%	2.2%	0.1%	9.4%
Wareham	3.8%	0.4%	0.0%	4.2%

cases, were so insignificant as to leave few traces in historical records, other than the records of the courts. Like the other towns in the county, Plymouth had an underclass that was highly litigious in nature. Thus, a number of its highly litigious residents also frequented the Court of General Sessions as criminal defendants. Nine of the 66, for instance, were indicted once, while Thomas Faunce was indicted twice; Samuel Clark, three times; Robert Finney, four times; Elisha Cobb, five times; and Quintin Crymble, seven times. As many as five of the town's highly litigious inhabitants may have been paupers who required public assistance. However, Plymouth's highly litigious residents also differed from similar groups elsewhere in that they included many of the town's leading men. Among the highly litigious were seven of the nine men who represented Plymouth at the General Court between 1725 and 1774, seven of the ten men who moderated the town meeting during the period, and three of the eight deacons of the First Church. In addition, fourteen of the 66 served the town in the office of selectman, and nine held commissions as justices of the peace, one of whom was also a judge of the Inferior Court of Common Pleas. The litigious also included two town clerks, two tax collectors, a militia captain, an overseer of the poor,[65] and one man, Nathaniel Goodwin, who served on the town's school committee and its committee to frame instructions for its representative at the General Court in reference to the Stamp Act.[66] In other words, it appears that a larger part of the governing elite of Plymouth than of those of other towns brought their disputes with their fellow townsmen to court rather than local community institutions.

In the end, the litigation pattern of Plymouth differed sharply from patterns in the nonlitigious towns. In Plymouth, about 3 percent of the people—many of whom were engaged directly or indirectly in commerce and were among the town's elite—took their disputes to court with great frequency, usually as plaintiffs and often with success.[67] In no other pre-Revolutionary town were so many leading citizens committed to judicial rather than ecclesiastical dispute resolution.

Scituate and Rochester: A Conjunction of Commerce and Religion

The two remaining towns in pre-Revolutionary Plymouth County, Scituate and Rochester, both had relatively high rates of intracommunity litigation. Scituate, for instance, had a total of 484 intratown cases between 1725 and 1774. However, it contained two separate parishes, and, on the basis of a 49-case sample in which all litigants were from the same parish in only 23 cases, it can be estimated that only 47 percent of Scituate's cases—227 cases in all—were intracommunity in nature.[68] Similarly, Rochester, which had a total of 411 intratown cases, contained three separate parishes, one of which was very large in size and hence ought to be treated as two separate communities roughly coterminous with the present town of Marion and the present community located at Rochester Center.[69] Wareham was a fifth subcommunity within the town of Rochester until it became a separate town in 1739. On the basis of a sample of 79 cases, in 37 of which all parties were from a single subcommunity, an estimate can be made that 47 percent of Rochester's intratown cases—193 cases in all—were of an intracommunity nature.[70]

In Scituate, commercial litigants—traders, maritime workers, and manufacturers—appeared in 42 percent of all cases, and in Rochester they appeared in 34 percent. When these commercial cases are subtracted, Scituate is left with an estimated total of 132 and Rochester with an estimated total of 127 noncommercial intracommunity cases during the half century from 1725 to 1774.[71] Table 3.6 adds this data for Scituate and Rochester to data presented for the county's twelve other towns in table 3.4. As table 3.6 shows, Scituate and Rochester had rates of noncommercial intracommunity litigation below the rates of four other towns, and thus the difference between their overall rates of litigation and the rates of less litigious towns can be accounted for, at least in part, by the larger amount of commercial litigation in Scituate and Rochester.

Litigation patterns in the two towns, however, were in fact more complex. Scituate, like Pembroke and Hanover, its neighbors to the west, had many Quaker residents who appeared with some frequency in intratown litigation.[72] Indeed,

TABLE 3.6 Fourteen Towns: Noncommercial Intracommunity Cases, 1725–1774

	Total Cases	*Cases per Year per 1,000 Residents*
Pembroke	226	3.21
Plymouth	208	1.91
Hanover	90	1.66
Duxbury	77	1.47
Rochester[73]	127	1.31
Plympton	85	1.22
Scituate[74]	132	1.06
Kingston	34	0.91
Marshfield	38	0.66
Middleboro	112	0.66
Bridgewater	120	0.61
Abington	28	0.44
Wareham	8	0.44
Halifax	5	0.22

they took part in 44 of its 484 intratown cases, or 9 percent of the total. This is, of course, a significantly lower rate of appearance than the corresponding rates of 49 percent in Pembroke and 32 in Hanover. Nonetheless, it must be determined whether the 44 Quaker cases account for much of the difference between Scituate's rate of noncommercial intracommunity litigation and lower rates in other towns. In fact, the Quaker cases account for almost none of the difference because three-fourths of them, or 33 out of the total of 44, were commercial in character and hence are already not included in the total of 281 noncommercial cases. There remain only 11 Quaker cases of a noncommercial nature. Because subtraction of these from the remaining Scituate totals would have a negligible impact on the town's overall profile, it must be concluded that the presence of Quakers in the parishes of Scituate, unlike their presence in the towns of Hanover and Pembroke, did little to increase the amount of noncommercial intracommunity litigation occurring in those parishes.

The same cannot be said about Rochester. During the sixteen years from 1725 to 1740, it had a total of 238 intratown cases, or an average of 14.88 per year—an unusually high rate of intratown litigation. Eighty-three of the cases, or 35 percent of the total, involved at least one Quaker party,[75] but that still leaves 155 cases, or 9.69 per year, in which Quakers were not parties.

Two factors that have already been considered largely explain the high rate: the number of commercial cases and the fact that the town of Rochester consisted of several separate, distinct communities. There remains, however, one more event that should be taken into account: a schism during the late 1730s in Rochester's Second Parish, which today constitutes the town of Mattapoisett. It appears from the church records that the people of Mattapoisett were engaged in a major theological dispute when their parish was established in 1737. As a result, they were unable to select a minister for their new church until 1740.[76] Indeed, it was not until 1742 that the majority of "the Second Chh of Christ in Rochester met together again with some of those their Brethren who [had] dissented from it in ordr to come to a mutual Aggreemt respecting their old Difference," and only then, after five years of conflict, did the two sides make "their Interchangible acknowlegmts of their Faults one to another & therein mutually agree . . . to bury all the sd former Difference in oblivion."[77] During the interval, the community had seethed with conflict and division. In short, the church in Mattapoisett parish may have broken down during the 1730s as an institution capable of assisting individuals in resolving disputes, and, as a result, they may have found it necessary to resort to the courts.

In fact, on the basis of a sample of Mattapoisett cases that is suggestive, although too small to be completely reliable, it appears that more than half of all pre-Revolutionary intraparish litigation in Mattapoisett occurred during the schism.[78] Accordingly, it can be guessed that schism in one Congregational parish contributed, along with the presence of religious dissenters and the appearance in court of commercial litigants, to the high pre-1740 intracommunity litigation rate of Rochester. Hence the litigation pattern of Rochester combined aspects of the patterns of Middleboro, Pembroke, and Plymouth. To a lesser extent, the pattern of Scituate also contained elements found in those of several other towns. Given the high litigation rates of Scituate and Rochester, it is not surprising that the percentages of their populations involved in litigation remained comparatively high at every level of frequency. Table 3.7 illustrates this by adding statistics for Scituate and Rochester to statistics presented in table 3.5. Scituate and Rochester also appear as unusually litigious in table 3.8, which summarizes data on the number of cases in each town in which no highly litigious individual participated.

Finally, when data on specific highly litigious individuals in Scituate are examined, it appears that the town had a pattern closer to that of Plymouth than any of the nonlitigious towns. As was true in all towns in the county, a large portion of all Scituate residents appearing in intratown litigation on 8 or more occasions also appeared in court as criminal defendants: a total of nine out of Scituate's thirty-one highly litigious individuals. More to the point, eight of the thirty-one held major town offices such as selectman, moderator, treasurer, and representative to the General Court;[79] four of the

TABLE 3.7 Fourteen Towns: Percentage of Frequency of Appearances by Residents, 1725–1774

	One or Two Times	*Three–Seven Times*	*Eight or More Times*	*At Any Time*
Abington	4.3%	0.6%	0.0%	4.9%
Bridgewater	6.8%	2.1%	0.4%	9.3%
Duxbury	10.4%	3.0%	0.5%	13.9%
Halifax	2.5%	0.2%	0.0%	2.7%
Hanover	7.0%	2.7%	1.0%	10.7%
Kingston	5.9%	2.3%	0.5%	8.7%
Marshfield	7.1%	1.0%	0.0%	8.1%
Middleboro	8.4%	2.1%	0.7%	11.2%
Pembroke	10.9%	3.1%	1.1%	15.1%
Plymouth	14.8%	6.2%	3.0%	24.0%
Plympton	7.1%	2.2%	0.1%	9.4%
Rochester	11.1%	4.1%	1.1%	16.3%
Scituate	10.5%	4.0%	1.2%	15.7%
Wareham	3.8%	0.4%	0.0%	4.2%

eight also held judicial office, three as justices of the peace and one, John Cushing, as a member of the Superior Court of Judicature. Hence, about one-fourth of Scituate's highly litigious residents can be identified as members of the town's elite. This is a somewhat higher proportion than in the nonlitigious towns but a somewhat lower one than in Plymouth. Unfortunately, the absence of many town records and of any reliable town history precludes the gathering of information about highly litigious individuals in Rochester.[80]

Thus, Scituate and Rochester, which were microcosms of the entire county in that they were coastal towns having extensive agrarian hinterlands, also tended to mirror the county

TABLE 3.8 Fourteen Towns: Intratown Cases Not Involving Highly Litigious Residents, 1725–1774

	Total Cases	*Cases per Year per 1,000 Residents*
Abington	44	0.70
Bridgewater	244	1.24
Duxbury	98	1.87
Halifax	9	0.40
Hanover	71	1.31
Kingston	40	1.08
Marshfield	61	1.06
Middleboro	201	1.18
Pembroke	98	1.39
Plymouth	171	1.57
Plympton	108	1.55
Rochester	167	1.72
Scituate	256	2.06
Wareham	12	0.66

as a whole in their litigation patterns. Most factors that led individually to the breakdown of communal dispute-resolving mechanisms elsewhere in the county also led in combination to their breakdown in these two towns.

Summary

The ultimate aim of the discussion above of the patterns of intratown litigation in the fourteen colonial towns of Plymouth County is comparison of the circumstances under which residents in those towns turned to their local congregation for the resolution of their disputes with the circumstances under which they brought their disputes to formal legal institutions. The overall pattern that emerges is not surprising. In most communities, it appears that people usually brought their disputes with their neighbors to the church. There were, however, four circumstances in which cases might be taken to court. The first was when one of the parties was a troublemaker, an outcast, or some other sort of person who was not amenable to moral suasion by the church and the local community. The second was when religious dissent was present in a neighborhood; then, interdenominational cases would be taken to the courts. The third was the existence of schism within a Congregational church of the sort occurring in Mattapoisett in the 1730s and Middleboro in the 1740s—schism that apparently had a paralytic effect upon the congregation's capacity to resolve disputes. The fourth was the presence of one or more commercial litigants in a dispute.

The reasons why these four factors would result in an increase in litigation in the courts will be discussed later. Meanwhile, a comparison will be made of the pre-Revolutionary litigation patterns discussed in this chapter with patterns that arose after the Revolution in an effort to determine the extent to which the same four factors or, perhaps, other factors seem to account for differences in the rate of litigiousness.

4 The Changing Statistical Pattern of Post-Revolutionary Litigation

As discussed earlier, Plymouth's courts during the provincial period had played a small role in the resolution of intracommunity disputes in the majority of the county's towns. However, during the last decade of the eighteenth century, the judiciary's role began to increase. By the 1810s the courts had become, for almost every case that could not be resolved informally, the only institution that was available to adjudicate a dispute. Statistically, this transition is evidenced by a large increase in intratown and intracommunity litigation that in the mid-eighteenth century had frequently been settled by nonjudicial institutions. This increase will be analyzed by comparing statistical data for the period 1781–1825 with the data that has already been presented for the period 1725–74. The ultimate objective will be to address in the final chapter the changed social conditions that led to the collapse of the church as an adjudicatory institution. Although the full rise in intratown and intracommunity litigation did not occur immediately after 1781, that year nevertheless constitutes a convenient point at which to begin analysis of the rise, partly because the courts heard very few cases during six years of the War of Independence—namely, 1775 to 1780[1]—and partly because, when the courts did again begin in 1781 to hear a large number of cases, the statistical pattern of the litigation before them was somewhat different from what it had been in years prior to 1775.

The General Increase in Intratown Litigation

The first fact that strikes the student of post-independence patterns of litigation is the substantial increase occurring in the total number of intratown cases. During the half century before independence, there had been a total of 3,562 intratown cases spread among all of the county's towns, or an average of 71.24 cases per year. In the forty-five years from 1781 to 1825, on the other hand, 4,840 intratown cases were brought to court, an average of 107.56 per year. This represents an increase of 51 percent in the average number of cases per year.

Of course, the county's population also rose between 1765 and 1820[2]—at an almost identical rate of 52 percent. Accordingly, it is tempting to conclude that the corresponding increase in intratown litigation over this period resulted entirely from population growth. That conclusion, however, would be inappropriate. Although population is surely a major determinant of the amount of litigation occurring in a society, it is not the sole determinant. Other obvious elements are economic conditions, jurisdictional limitations, and the costs of going to court. Thus, before simply concluding that intratown litigation was rising in proportion to population, it is necessary to consider whether the total quantity of litigation in the county—both intratown and intertown—was similarly rising.

In fact, litigation in general was not rising. In the half century before the Revolution, residents of Plymouth County commenced a total of 8,360 lawsuits against each other in the Court of Common Pleas for the county, an average of 167.20 cases per year. Between 1781 and 1825, residents of the county commenced 8,500 such suits in the Court of Common Pleas. This represented an average of 188.89 cases per year, or an increase of only 13 percent.[3] Accordingly, intratown litigation came to constitute an increasingly large portion of total litigation in the county. Whereas residents of Plymouth prior to the Revolution brought 43 percent of their intracounty lawsuits against residents of their own town, they brought 57 percent of them against fellow townsmen in the post-Revolutionary period.

The increase in intratown litigation manifested itself in nearly every town in the county. In six towns, the average rate of intratown litigation more than doubled. Table 4.1 presents the data for these towns. Five other towns experienced smaller increases in their intratown litigation rate. Table 4.2 presents the data for them. In two other towns, Hanover and Pembroke, intratown litigation rates for the entire post-Revolutionary period were slightly lower than the rates for the entire pre-Revolutionary period, falling in Hanover from 3.36 to 2.96 cases per year, and in Pembroke from 6.20 to 5.60 cases per year. This apparent post-Revolutionary decline in intratown litigation is due, however, to the relatively large quantity of litigation generated prior to 1740 by the presence of Quakers in the two towns. Thus, if intratown litigation rates for the thirty-five year period immediately before the Revolution, 1740–74, are compared with corresponding rates for the period 1781–1825, a rise in the rates for both towns occurs. In Hanover, the rate rises slightly from 2.66 cases per year for the period 1740–74 to 2.96 cases per year for the post-Revolutionary period, an increase of 11 percent. In Pembroke, the rate rises from 4.60 to 5.60 cases per year, a gain of 22 percent. There remains only one town in the county,

TABLE 4.1 Six Towns: Frequency of Intratown Litigation, 1725–1774 and 1781–1825

	Cases per Year, 1725–1774	*Cases per Year, 1781–1825*	*Percent Increase*
Wareham	0.33	1.67	406.1%
Halifax	0.22	0.98	345.5%
Abington	0.88	3.58	306.8%
Middleboro	8.78	22.82	159.9%
Bridgewater	8.10	20.24	149.9%
Plympton	2.36	5.16	118.6%

TABLE 4.2 Five Towns: Frequency of Intratown Litigation, 1725–1774 and 1781–1825

	Cases per Year, 1725–1774	*Cases per Year, 1781–1825*	*Percent Increase*
Duxbury	2.70	4.18	54.8%
Marshfield	1.22	1.82	49.2%
Kingston	1.53	2.20	43.8%
Rochester	8.22	11.00	33.8%
Plymouth	17.82	18.87	5.9%

Scituate, that did not participate in the general rise in intratown litigation taking place in the post-Revolutionary period. Indeed, in Scituate, the intratown litigation rate fell sharply from 9.68 to 6.58 cases per year, a decline of 32 percent.

The rise in intratown litigation appears to have come about in two or three separate stages. Immediately after the Revolution, during the six-year period from 1781 to 1786, the average number of intratown cases per year in the entire county rose from the pre-Revolutionary rate of 71.24 to a new high of 100.20. This rise in the number of intratown cases was paralleled, however, by a rise in the overall number of cases that Plymouth County residents instituted against each other in the Court of Common Pleas. That figure rose from the pre-Revolutionary average of 167.20 cases per year to a new average of 213.33 cases. As a result, the percentage of Plymouth County litigation that was intratown in nature did not change substantially between the pre-Revolutionary era and the immediate post-Revolutionary years. Before the Revolution, Plymouth County residents instituted 43 percent of all their lawsuits against fellow townsmen; during the years 1781–86, the figure rose to 47 percent.

It is worthwhile to pause at this juncture to consider in greater depth the causes of this initial increase. The traditional explanation for the 1780s rise is that creditors were imposing heavy pressures upon debtors through the judicial process to recover their debts during a period of difficult economic times.[4] Undoubtedly, this tells part of the story. However, there are additional complexities. For the 1780s saw not only an increase in total litigation and in intratown litigation, but an even more striking increase in the number of lawsuits instituted by lower-class plaintiffs against upper-class defendants.

Using the 10-percent sample of all Plymouth County cases,[5] men were identified as upper class if they were esquires, gentlemen, or merchants and as lower class if they were farmers, seamen, transportation workers, or laborers.[6] By this measure, upper-class litigants in the pre-Revolutionary period sued those below them on the social scale 4.2 times more frequently than those below sued them.[7] Intratown litigation statistics[8] from the pre-Revolutionary period replicate this pattern. They show that upper-class individuals appeared as plaintiffs 3.5 times more frequently than they appeared as defendants.[9]

Because it is not clear that the above definitions of upper and lower class are the most appropriate ones, an analysis was made of the frequency with which litigants from the three lowest classes—seamen, transportation workers, and laborers—appeared as defendants in suits at the hands of the three upper classes and of farmers compared with the frequency with which they appeared as plaintiffs against those same classes. As the following discussion will show, it makes little difference which definition is adopted. According to the 10-percent sample, the three lowest classes in the pre-Revolutionary period appeared as defendants 3.7 times more frequently against the four other classes than they appeared as plaintiffs.[10] Similarly, in pre-Revolutionary intratown litigation, the three lowest classes appeared 3.4 times more frequently as defendants than as plaintiffs.[11]

The decade of the 1780s witnessed a significant change in these ratios. According to the 10-percent sample, the three upper classes appeared as plaintiffs against the four lower classes rather than as defendants only 1.6 rather than 4.2 times more frequently.[12] In intratown cases, the three upper classes appeared as plaintiffs only 1.4 times more frequently than as defendants.[13] The three lowest classes—seamen, transportation workers, and laborers—also enjoyed far more favorable ratios as against the four higher classes. According to the 10-percent sample, the three lowest classes appeared as defendants against the other four classes only 2.2 rather than 3.7 times more frequently than they appeared as plaintiffs. This sample, however, is too small to be statistically significant.[14] But intratown litigation statistics, which are derived from a compilation of all cases rather than a sample, show an even more striking shift. According to the intratown statistics, the three lowest classes appeared as plaintiffs against the four other classes in 41 cases during the 1780s and as defendants in only 19—a sharp reversal from the pre-Revolutionary pattern in which those three classes had appeared 3.4 times more frequently as defendants than as plaintiffs.

The lower classes, defined in either of the two ways above, were bringing a larger portion of all litigation during the 1780s than they had brought prior to the Revolution. In fact, the added number of suits instituted by lower-class plaintiffs accounted for much of the general increase in litigation that eventuated during the 1780s. It will be recalled that Plymouth County residents had brought an average of 167.20 cases per year prior to the Revolution and that between 1781 and 1786 the average increased by 46.13 cases to 213.33 per year. This increase cannot be accounted for by suits in which litigants from the three upper classes were plaintiffs against a member of one of the four lower classes, for such cases declined during the 1780s by an average of four cases per year, from 32.00 cases per year before the Revolution to 28.00 during the 1780s. However, suits in which the four lower classes appeared as plaintiffs against the three upper classes rose by an average of 10.40 per year—from 7.60 per year prior to the Revolution to 18.00 per year during the 1780s. This 10.40-case-per-year increase accounted for about one-fourth of the total increase in litigation during the 1780s. Similarly, in intratown litigation, the upper classes did not substantially increase the number of cases that they brought as plaintiffs: the number of cases they brought against those who were lower on the social ladder rose only from 10.10 to 10.80 per year. However, the number of cases in which the four upper classes were sued by the three lower classes rose from 2.92 to 7.80 cases per year. This increase of 4.88 cases per year accounted for approximately one-sixth of the total increase in post-Revolutionary intratown litigation.

Thus, contrary to the standard accounts, the 1780s was not simply a decade in which the rich used the judicial process to oppress the poor, at least in Plymouth County. On the contrary, those who can be identified as upper class by either definition did not increase their rate of litigation against their inferiors during the decade, whereas those who can be identified as lower class did sue their betters more often. The reasons for this increase in lower-class litigiousness are not central to this study. Nonetheless, two possible explanations may be suggested. One is that an egalitarian impulse stemming from the Revolution lessened traditional deference and thereby facilitated the commencement of lawsuits against the elite.[15] A second and not necessarily inconsistent explanation may be that the Revolution produced an unsettling effect upon the membership of the upper classes, leading to a period in which some old established members of the elite fell from the top and new entrants took their place. If this in fact occurred,[16] it would not be strange that an unstable elite in the post-Revolutionary era was more easily sued than the stable pre-Revolutionary elite. In short, the general rise in litigation during the 1780s may have been the result of a variety of factors, among them hard times, a refusal by creditors to exercise forebearance, an egalitarian impulse, and a temporary instability in the class structure.

Whatever the causes of the rise in litigation may have been, that rise came to a sudden halt in 1787, at least with respect to litigation in the Court of Common Pleas. The immediate cause of the halt was a series of statutes that took jurisdiction over cases involving small amounts of money away from Common Pleas and gave it to justices of the peace,[17] who kept no systematic records. The result of the legislation was that in

1787 only 36 intratown cases were recorded in the record books of the Court of Common Pleas out of a total of 64 cases commenced by Plymouth County residents against each other. Of course, this sharp recorded drop in litigation may have been nothing more than a clerical aberration resulting from the failure of the records to reveal the total number of cases commenced in all courts, including the justices' courts. The long-term drop in recorded litigation that began in 1787 may not, however, have been entirely the result of jurisdictional changes, given the restoration of much of Common Pleas' jurisdiction by 1790.[18] The long-term drop may, instead, have reflected a stabilization of the class structure and the end of the depression that had contributed to the earlier litigation explosion.[19] Whether the total amount of litigation actually rose or fell is, however, neither important nor capable of being determined.

What is important is that, if total litigation actually fell, intratown litigation nonetheless rose after 1787, and, if total litigation rose, then intratown litigation rose more rapidly. During the nineteen-year period from 1787 to 1805, residents of the county brought a total of 1,453 intratown cases in Common Pleas, or an average of 76.47 cases per year. This represented an increase of 5.23 cases over the pre-Revolutionary average of 71.24 cases per year. This small increase was significant, however, because the total amount of recorded litigation commenced by Plymouth County residents against each other fell to 2,480 cases during the nineteen-year period, for an average of 130.53 cases per year compared to the pre-Revolutionary average of 167.20 cases per year. Intratown cases accordingly came to constitute 59 percent of intracounty litigation, compared to the pre-Revolutionary average of 43 percent.

This increase in intratown litigation was followed by another, beginning in 1805–6. In 1804, a total of 54 intratown cases were recorded in the judgment rolls of the Court of Common Pleas. That number rose to 94 in 1805, 118 in 1806, 105 in 1807, and 190 in 1808. During the twenty-year period from 1806 to 1825, there was a total of 2,786 intratown cases, or an average of 139.30 cases per year. Total litigation, however, also rose to 4,740 cases, an average of 237 cases per year. As a result, although the number of intratown cases increased, intratown litigation remained at 59 percent of the total.

The return of the overall rate of recorded litigation to pre-Revolutionary levels beginning in the 1790s was accompanied by a return to a pre-Revolutionary pattern of class distribution. According to the 10-percent sample, the three upper classes sued the four lower ones 3.4 times more frequently than the lower ones sued them during the period from 1791 to 1825,[20] while the three lowest classes again began to appear against the four upper classes 3.7 times more frequently as defendants than as plaintiffs.[21] In intratown litigation, the three upper classes appeared as plaintiffs 3.1 times more often than they appeared as defendants during the period 1791–1825,[22] while the three lowest classes similarly appeared 3.1 times more frequently as defendants than as plaintiffs.[23] After 1790, in sum, the lower classes ceased to sue the upper classes almost as frequently as they were sued by them—the pattern of the 1780s. The lower classes again found themselves on the defensive end of litigation about three times more frequently than on the complaining end—the pattern of the pre-Revolutionary period.

Thus, after an unsettled and statistically anomalous decade in the 1780s, litigation patterns—with one exception—returned to their pre-Revolutionary norms in the 1790s. The exception was that recorded intratown litigation never fell back to pre-Revolutionary levels, but instead remained closer to its figure for the 1780s. And, when examined as a percentage of total litigation, intratown litigation rose for the first time from under 50 to nearly 60 percent of all cases. In other words, a pattern evolved in which all litigation rose in the years immediately following the American Revolution, but then fell back by 1790 to approximately its pre-Revolutionary rates. Either as a residual effect of this initial post-Revolutionary rise or as a result of independent forces, however, the percentage of all litigation that was intratown in nature was more than 10 points higher in the 1790s than it previously had been. The percentage remained at the new rate throughout the period under study. Moreover, the total quantity of both intertown and intratown litigation began to rise sharply in 1805. Even these statistics, however, do not reveal the full extent of the rise in litigation between neighbors for they do not disclose how intratown litigation in the larger towns came to consist increasingly of litigation between residents of the smaller communities of which those towns were comprised rather than between residents of different communities. Accordingly, patterns of litigation within the individual towns must next be examined.

The Transformation of Intracommunity Litigation Patterns in Ten Towns

Ten of Plymouth County's fourteen towns—Abington, Bridgewater (including North Bridgewater, East Bridgewater, and West Bridgewater, which were incorporated in the early 1820s), Duxbury, Halifax, Kingston, Middleboro, Pembroke (including Hanson, which was carved out of it in 1820), Plympton (including Carver, which was set off in 1790), Rochester, and Wareham—experienced a series of dramatic changes in the patterns of intracommunity litigation during the first decade of the nineteenth century. The first signs of change appeared in several towns as early as 1797, but the pattern of change was not fully consummated in all the towns until 1810. Different facets of the overall transformation occurred, of course, at different times in different towns, and it is impossible to date many of the changes precisely other than for purposes of convenience in analyzing statistical data. What is clear, however, is that, until the transformation began, each town's litigation pattern was similar to that of the nine nonlitigious towns of the pre-Revolutionary period, whereas, once the transformation was completed, each town manifested a pattern similar in most respects to that of pre-Revolutionary Plymouth.

One change—that in the rate of intracommunity litigation—can be analyzed only in the three largest towns: Bridgewater, Middleboro, and Rochester. As was seen in the analysis of their pre-Revolutionary litigation patterns, these towns were divided into a series of distinct subcommunities.[24] In Bridgewater and Middleboro and perhaps in Rochester, the percentage of intratown litigation that was of an intracommunity nature increased between the immediate post-Revolutionary period and the early nineteenth century.

Before the Revolution, only 37 percent of Middleboro's intratown litigation had been of an intracommunity nature. The remainder had been between residents of the different subcommunities into which the town was divided geographically. Until 1797, intracommunity litigation remained quite low; a sample of 37 cases from the years 1781–97 indicates that intracommunity cases amounted to only 22 percent of all intratown cases during that period. Assuming that this estimate is low in view of the corresponding pre-Revolutionary rate of 37 percent, it does suggest strongly that the rate of intracommunity litigation in Middleboro did not rise after the Revolution from its pre-Revolutionary rate.[25] Beginning in 1798, however, intracommunity litigation began to constitute a larger portion of Middleboro's intratown litigation than in the period 1781–97. A sample of 27 cases from the three-year period 1798–1800 indicates that 52 percent of the town's intratown litigation was intracommunity. Although this sample is too small to be accurate,[26] a larger sample of 157 cases for the entire period 1798–1825 indicates that 46 percent of that litigation was intracommunity.[27] On the basis of this latter sample, it can be estimated that 370 of Middleboro's 806 intratown cases from the period 1798–1825, or an average of 13.21 cases per year, were intracommunity cases.[28]

An even greater change apparently occurred in Bridgewater. Over the entire eighteenth century, intracommunity litigation amounted to slightly more than one-third of Bridgewater's intratown litigation: 36 percent prior to the Revolution; 37 percent between 1781 and 1786;[29] and 36 percent between 1787 and 1800.[30] After 1800, however, change began to set in. A sample of 35 cases for the decade 1801–10 suggests that intracommunity litigation rose to 60 percent of all intratown litigation during that decade, but this sample is too small to be very reliable.[31] A similar sample of 39 cases for the decade 1811–20 suggests that intracommunity litigation then jumped to 80 percent of intratown litigation. Although this sample is also too small to be completely reliable,[32] it is supported by data from the years 1822–25, the first four years after Bridgewater's division into four separate towns had been effected. During those four years, residents of the four new towns brought a total of 97 suits either against fellow townsmen or against residents of one of the other three towns; 81 of these cases, or 84 percent,[33] were brought against residents of the same community. Accordingly, it seems fair to estimate that after 1810 approximately 80 percent of Bridgewater's intratown cases were of an intracommunity nature and that this figure rose from approximately 37 to approximately 80 percent sometime between 1801 and 1810. Taken in conjunction with an increase beginning in 1797 in the total number of intratown cases, the rise in the percentage of those cases that were of an intracommunity nature makes it possible to estimate that, beginning in 1811, Bridgewater averaged about 22 intracommunity cases per year.

In the third town, Rochester, it is not clear whether a change took place in the proportion of intratown cases that were of an intracommunity nature. The difficulty stems from the impossibility of accumulating samples larger than 39 cases for the thirty years from 1781 to 1810 and 51 cases for the 15 years from 1811 to 1825. According to these two samples, intracommunity litigation rose from 16 out of 39 cases, or 41 percent of the total, prior to 1810, to 25 out of 51 cases, or 49 percent of the total, after 1811. These samples are too small, however, to measure accurately a mere 8-point rise in the rate of intracommunity litigation.[34] Although an increase of that or even greater magnitude may have occurred, as it did in Bridgewater and Middleboro, Rochester's rate of intracommunity litigation might as easily have remained constant during all of the post-Revolutionary period. For purposes of analysis in this section, I made a more conservative assumption that the percentage of intratown cases that were intracommunity in nature remained constant throughout the post-Revolutionary period[35] at 46 percent—a rate derived from a combined sample of 90 cases,[36] 41 of which were intracommunity. However, because intratown litigation began to increase sharply in 1803, a rise in intracommunity litigation—from an average of 2.31 to 7.02 cases per year—can be observed beginning that year.

Table 4.3 presents data on the average number of intracommunity cases per year in all ten towns for four different time periods: pre-Revolutionary, 1781–86, the period from 1787 to the year before each town's litigation rate began to increase, and the period from the year after each town's increase was completed until 1825. Intracommunity litigation in Bridgewater, Middleboro, and Rochester is defined as a percentage of each town's intratown litigation. This percentage changed in Bridgewater and Middleboro, but remained constant in Rochester. Because of the small size of the remaining seven towns under analysis, no attempt was made to break them down into separate communities. Instead, their intratown litigation is assumed to have all been of an intracommunity nature.[37] Table 4.3 shows that every town except Kingston experienced an increase, often dramatic, in intracommunity litigation between the pre-Revolutionary and the

TABLE 4.3 Ten Towns: Frequency of Intracommunity Litigation, 1725–1825

	Cases per Year, 1725–1774	*Cases per Year, 1781–1786*	*Cases per Year, 1787–Rise*	*Cases per Year, Rise–1825*
Abington[38]	0.88	1.33	0.80	5.83
Bridgewater[39]	2.92	9.93	3.10	22.08
Duxbury[38]	2.70	3.67	2.67	5.25
Halifax[40]	0.22	0.83	0.28	1.62
Kingston[41]	1.53	1.00	1.16	3.35
Middleboro[42]	3.24	3.37	2.42	12.93
Pembroke[40]	4.60	4.83	2.67	8.29
Plympton[40]	2.08	4.50	2.78	7.38
Rochester[43]	3.86	4.56	2.31	7.02
Wareham[44]	0.33	2.33	0.30	2.10

immediate post-Revolutionary periods. It then shows that, in the period beginning in 1787, every town experienced a rate of intracommunity litigation that was either lower than or approximately equal to its pre-Revolutionary rate. Most significantly, the table shows that in the final period beginning around the turn of the century every town underwent a more than twofold increase in the amount of intracommunity litigation, except Duxbury, where intracommunity litigation rose by 97 percent.

As intracommunity litigation increased in each town in the years around 1800, its pattern of litigation became more like that of Plymouth in that parties engaged in commerce and manufacturing tended to appear in an increasing percentage of the cases. Table 4.4 presents data on this increase in the commercial nature of litigation by listing for each town the percentage of cases in which commercial litigants appeared between 1781 and the beginning of the town's litigation rise and the percentage in which they appeared between the end of the rise and 1825. As Table 4.4 shows, eight towns experienced an increase of 10 percentage points or more in their rate of commercial litigation between the prerise and postrise period. The only towns that did not experience such an increase were Duxbury, where litigation had already become heavily commercial in the immediate post-Revolutionary period, and Halifax, where there were only two commercial cases in the entire forty-five years under analysis, one in 1785 and the other in 1822.

Another way in which the intracommunity litigation patterns of the ten towns became like that of pre-Revolutionary Plymouth was that a small group of town leaders began to appear in intratown cases with great frequency. Each of the ten towns will now be considered.

In the pre-Revolutionary period in Middleboro, 24 indi-

TABLE 4.4 Ten Towns: Percentage of Frequency of Commercial Litigation, 1781–1825

	Commercial Cases 1781–Rise[45]	*Commercial Cases Rise–1825*
Abington	20.0%	42.1%
Bridgewater	15.5%	29.4%
Duxbury	74.6%	73.8%
Halifax	10.0%	2.9%
Kingston	30.8%	62.3%
Middleboro	11.2%	31.9%
Pembroke	28.2%	38.2%
Plympton	16.0%	44.4%
Rochester	26.5%	40.7%
Wareham	20.0%	35.1%

viduals who came to court on 8 or more occasions—a mere 6 percent of all those appearing in its intratown litigation—had accounted for fully 32 percent of all appearances. A pattern in which a few individuals accounted for an even greater percentage of all appearances persisted from 1798 to 1825, over which time 51 individuals, or 9 percent of all those appearing, accounted for 47 percent of all appearances. From 1781 to 1797, however, the pattern was different. Only 4 individuals, who constituted 2 percent of all litigants, put in 8 or more appearances, and those 4 accounted for a mere 9 percent of all appearances.

This scarcity of litigious individuals from 1781 to 1797 is not a statistical fluke resulting from the shortness of the interval. If the entire forty-five years of post-Revolutionary Middleboro litigation is examined as a single unit, there are a total of 59 litigants who made a total of 8 or more appearances. Only 5 of them—the 4 previously noted and 1 other man who appeared 7 times prior to 1798—made the majority of their appearances during the first seventeen years of the period. The other 54 litigants, who made the majority of their appearances from 1798 on, made very few prior to that year. One man, who appeared 10 times from 1798 on, put in a total of 7 appearances prior to that time. Another who appeared 11 times in the latter period did so 6 times in the earlier one. Of the remaining 52 post-1798 litigants, 15 of whom appeared 20 or more times beginning in 1798, none appeared more than 3 times prior to 1798, 4 appeared 3 times, 10 appeared twice, 7 appeared once, and the remaining 31 never appeared at all. It thus seems that a new breed of litigious people, largely absent from the town in the decade and a half following the Revolution, reappeared beginning in 1798.

This group differed from the comparable pre-Revolutionary one in an important respect. Few of those who were most litigious in pre-Revolutionary Middleboro had been members of the town's governing elite. After 1798, on the other hand, those who were most litigious probably constituted a large part of the town's elite, which began to assume an increasingly commercial cast. Thus, 9 of the 10 most litigious individuals in the post-1798 period were merchants; the other was a practicing attorney. This group of 10 included 6 justices of the peace, 4 of whom served the town in at least one house of the state legislature, while a fifth served as a general in the local militia. Of the larger body of 52 individuals who appeared in court 8 or more times between 1798 and 1825, 23 were merchants, 2 were lawyers, 2 were engaged in manufacturing, and 2 were in the construction business. These 29 men, who amounted to only 5 percent of all individuals appearing in post-1798 intratown litigation in Middleboro, accounted for 33 percent of all appearances. Among the 29 were 9 justices of the peace, 6 state legislators, 4 militia officers, 3 town officers, and 1 deacon of the first church.[46] It is also worth noting that only 4 of the highly litigious individuals—Benjamin Coombs, Jedediah Miller, Levi Pierce, and Peter H. Pierce—were ever the subjects of criminal indictments, on one occasion each.

Comparable changes occurred in Bridgewater. Prior to the Revolution, individuals making 8 or more appearances had constituted 4 percent of those appearing in intratown litigation, had accounted for 22 percent of all appearances, and had appeared in 37 percent of all the cases. Between 1781 and 1797, 10 men, who amounted to 3 percent of all litigants appearing in intratown suits, accounted for 17 percent of all appearances, appearing in 39 percent of all the cases—numbers similar to those for the pre-Revolutionary period. Beginning in 1798, however, 36 litigants—6 percent of the total—accounted for 29 percent of all appearances, an increase of about 10 percentage points, and appeared in 49 percent of all cases, also an increase of about 10 points.

As had been true in the case of Middleboro, those who appeared in intratown litigation in Bridgewater after 1798, unlike those who did so before the Revolution, increasingly tended to be the leaders of the town's rising commercial elite. Thus, out of the 36 Bridgewater litigants who made 8 or more appearances after 1798, only 8 were ever indicted on criminal charges. The one indicted most—on 3 occasions—was Ezra Kingman, who as a town selectman was by no means an outcast. At the same time, 20 of the 36 were merchants, 2 were manufacturers, 2 were justices of the peace, and 1 was a practicing attorney who later became a judge on the Court of Common Pleas. Among them, these 25 litigants who had strong occupational ties to commerce and the law accounted for 235 appearances, or 16 percent, of Bridgewater's post-1798 appearances.

The pattern of change in Rochester was roughly the same. During the entire 45 years after the Revolution, a total of 20 men who appeared in court at least 8 or more times accounted for 268 out of a total of 1,070 appearances. Among these 20 were 9 merchants, 1 mariner, 1 physician, and 2 deputy sheriffs—a group whose composition was similar to that of the groups in Bridgewater and Middleboro. Until 1796, these 20 men rarely appeared in court; in fact, they made only 41 appearances in 38 cases. Most of Rochester's intratown litigation up to 1796 was between parties who did not appear in court as many as 8 times during their lives: 68 out of Rochester's 106 cases, or 64 percent, involved only such non-litigious individuals. Beginning in 1797, however, these same 20 men made a total of 227 appearances in 183 cases; they failed to appear in only 206 out of 389 cases, or 53 percent of the total.

In Abington during the entire pre-Revolutionary period and the post-Revolutionary period up to 1801, there had never been a single litigant who had appeared as many as 8 times in intratown litigation. But, after 1802, there were 8 individuals who made 8 or more such appearances—accounting for 23 percent of all post-1802 appearances and appearing in 40 percent of all Abington cases. Four of these 8 individuals were merchants, 1 was an attorney who never practiced but instead engaged in the business of manufacturing tacks,[47] and another was a justice of the peace. Only one of the 8, the merchant Micah White, was ever indicted for a criminal offense. Moreover, these 8 litigious individuals, like their counterparts in Middleboro, were a new breed of men who appeared in intratown litigation almost exclusively after 1802. In fact, only

2 of the 8 ever appeared during 1781–1801, each making 1 appearance in 1800.

Duxbury was like Abington in that the 6 men who appeared 8 or more times in post-Revolutionary Duxbury intratown litigation also made the bulk of their appearances after 1802. The 6, all of whom were merchants and 2 of whom were also representatives to the General Court,[48] made 16 percent of all the appearances in Duxbury litigation. They appeared a total of 68 times, 25 times between 1781 and 1801 and 43 times from 1802 to 1825. Similarly, in Halifax, Robert Inglee, a yeoman who appeared in court 8 times, made all his appearances in the period beginning in 1805. In Kingston, the 2 who made a total of 8 or more appearances in post-Revolutionary intratown litigation made most of them after 1806. One of these men, James Sever, made all of his 13 appearances after 1810, and the other man, Jedediah Holmes, made 7 of his 19 appearances prior to 1800 and the remaining 12 beginning in 1806. Holmes, it should be noted, was a merchant who represented Kingston in both the state senate and the state house of representatives and who also served the Commonwealth as justice of the peace. Sever was a citizen of sufficient prominence to be elected twice to the key post of town meeting moderator.[49]

A similar pattern of change occurred in the next two towns, Pembroke and Plympton. The 7 men in Pembroke who made 8 or more appearances went to court 27 times from 1781 to 1804 and 63 times thereafter. They appeared in 21 of 77 cases prior to 1805, or 27 percent of the total, and in 73 of 175 cases thereafter, or 42 percent of the total. One of these 7, Kilborn Whitman, was a lawyer who became a judge of the Court of Common Pleas but still remained sufficiently active in town affairs to be elected to ten terms as the town's representative to the General Court. Three of the other 6 men were manufacturers. Two of them, Isaac Barker and Samuel McFarland, were the only individuals among the 7 ever to be accused of a criminal offense; Barker, however, remained sufficiently prominent and respected in town affairs to be elected three times as representative to the General Court.[50] In Plympton, where 10 men made 8 or more appearances, the bulk of their appearances began to occur in 1805. From 1781 to 1804, they made only 24 appearances in 23 out of 76 cases, or 30 percent of the total. From 1805 to 1825, on the other hand, these 10 men made 170 appearances in 67 out of 156 cases, or 43 percent of the total. Most of these individuals seem to have been town leaders. One of them, Gideon Bradford, was a deputy sheriff who also served the town as a selectman, as town meeting moderator, and as representative to the General Court. Six others were merchants. Two of them, Ellis Wright and Isaac Wright, who were each the subject of one criminal indictment, were the only ones among the 10 ever to be indicted, but Isaac Wright, at least, remained sufficiently prominent and respected to be chosen as a selectman and as town meeting moderator. A third merchant, Jonathan Parker, also held office as a selectman, as town treasurer, and as representative to the General Court.[51] In sum, in both Pembroke and Plympton, the rise in intratown litigation that began in 1805 was accompanied by a change in the nature of the parties coming to court. Beginning that year, a small number of politically active men who often earned their livelihoods from trade and manufacturing began to appear in an increasingly large portion of the two towns' litigation. Finally, in Wareham, Curtis Tobey, a merchant, town clerk, and justice of the peace,[52] was the only person to appear more than 8 times in Wareham's intratown litigation; he made all his appearances after 1797.

Thus, in ten of the fourteen towns situated in Plymouth

County at the end of the Revolution, as well as in all the new towns created from 1790 to 1825, a uniform course of change can be discerned. In all the towns, intracommunity litigation rose sharply sometime during the last four years of the eighteenth century and the first decade of the nineteenth. Furthermore, as litigation rose, it took on an increasingly commercial cast in eight of the towns. In all the towns, litigation increasingly came to be a special province of a small number of often politically active individuals. In other words, litigation in the ten towns between 1797 and 1810 assumed the pattern of litigation that had been confined to the town of Plymouth in the pre-Revolutionary period—a pattern marked by large amounts of intracommunity litigation of a commercial nature in which a small portion of the entire community was heavily engaged. It is now time to turn to Plymouth to ascertain what happened to the pattern there during the post-Revolutionary period.

Increased Citizen Participation in Litigation in Plymouth

In general, the pattern of litigation in the town of Plymouth tended to remain much the same after the Revolution as it had been before. The average number of intratown cases per year rose slightly from 17.82 to 18.87. Commercial litigants, who had appeared in 77 percent of the pre-Revolutionary intratown cases, appeared in 62 percent of those arising after the Revolution. A large part of the intratown litigation also involved a small portion of its residents both before and after the Revolution. In the latter period, 595 separate individuals appeared in the town's 849 intratown cases, and made a total of 2,095 appearances. Sixty-seven, or 11 percent, of those individuals accounted for 1,034, or 49 percent of all appearances. Finally, as had also been the case before the Revolution, the majority of these individuals made their living, in whole or in part, through commercial, manufacturing, professional, or governmental careers. Among the 67, there were 24 merchants, 6 manufacturers, 2 seamen, 2 men in the construction business, 2 physicians, 1 engineer, 3 justices of the peace, and the county sheriff.

When the long-term pattern of Plymouth's litigation is analyzed, few lasting changes are apparent. Only cyclical fluctuations emerge, often occurring at intervals quite different from those during which the county's other towns experienced change. For example, between 1781 and 1786, when the others were undergoing large increases in their intratown litigation, Plymouth showed a total of 113 cases—an average of 18.83 per year, only slightly higher than the pre-Revolutionary average of 17.82 cases per year. During the next ten years, 1787–96, when litigation elsewhere fell sharply, Plymouth had a total of 184 intratown cases, or 18.40 cases per year. This was about the same average as for 1781–86. During the next eleven years, 1797–1807, when litigation in the ten towns previously considered was again beginning to rise steeply, Plymouth's was falling to a total of 152 cases, or an average of 13.82 per year. Between 1808, when Plymouth had 26 intratown cases, and 1817, when it had 32 cases, the town did have some very high yearly totals, such as 47 cases in 1810, 46 in 1812, and 49 in 1813, but after 1817 its rate of intratown litigation again declined sharply to an average of 11.00 cases per year for the eight years from 1818 to 1825.

However, one significant change began to occur in 1797, the year in which litigation patterns also began to change in several other towns. From 1781 to 1796, individuals who came to court at least 8 or more times during their lives had accounted for the bulk of the town's litigation. They appeared in 257 of the town's 297 intratown cases, or 87 percent of the total. A similar pattern had prevailed during the half century before the Revolution, when individuals who came to court 8 or more times appeared in 720 of the town's 891 cases—81 percent of the total. Of course, the absolute number of individuals making 8 or more appearances was small: there were only 66 such litigants during the entire fifty years before the Revolution and 67 during the entire forty-five years after. If cases involving these very few highly litigious people were excluded from the data, only a small number of cases would remain: 171, or an average of 3.42 per year during the half century before the Revolution, and 40, or an average of 2.50 per year, during the sixteen years after. This shows that, although there may have been a large amount of intratown litigation in Plymouth, the habit of taking disputes to court was not widespread, but was confined to a small segment of the entire population. Until 1796, most residents of the town settled their disputes without recourse to the courts, even though the few individuals who did come to court brought an immense number of cases with them.

In 1797, all this began to change. During the last four years of the eighteenth century, the 67 most litigious individuals of the post-Revolutionary period appeared in only 38 of the town's 76 intratown cases, or exactly half the total. During the entire twenty-nine years from 1797 to 1825 they appeared in 327 out of 554 cases, or 59 percent of the total. This left 227 cases, or an average of 7.83 cases per year, in which only less litigious individuals appeared. This represented a threefold rise over the average of 2.50 per year during 1781–96. In short, as was true in the ten other towns in the county, litigation with one's neighbor, formerly a rare event for most residents of the town of Plymouth, became much more common during the last four years of the eighteenth century and the first twenty-five years of the nineteenth.

This threefold "increase" in Plymouth's intratown litigation was far greater than the increase in the town's population over the corresponding period of time and was not matched by any equivalent rise in intertown litigation commenced by town residents. Indeed, the number of suits brought by residents of the town of Plymouth against residents of the county's other towns fell sharply in the post-Revolutionary period. Prior to the Revolution, it will be recalled, plaintiffs from the town of Plymouth had commenced a total of 2,360 lawsuits; of these, 891 were brought against other inhabitants of the town of Plymouth. This left a total of 1,469, or 29.38 cases per year, that were brought against residents of other towns in the county. Between 1781 and 1825, on the other hand, Plymouth plaintiffs brought 1,070 lawsuits, of which 849 were against other residents of the town. This left only 221 cases, or an average of 4.91 per year, brought against residents of other towns. This comparatively low rate of litigation between Plymouth plaintiffs and out-of-town defendants began at the outset of the post-Revolutionary period and, as far as the 10-percent sample indicates, remained a constant phenomenon throughout the forty-five years that followed.

Citizens of the town of Plymouth, in conclusion, unlike others throughout the county, did not become more litigious in the post-Revolutionary period; on the contrary, they became substantially less litigious. Beginning in 1797, however, litigation between neighbors, previously a rare phenomenon for most residents of the town, became a significantly more widespread one, just as it did in ten other towns in the county.

The Stagnant Northeast: Hanover, Marshfield, and Scituate

In three towns in the northeast corner of the county—Hanover, Marshfield, and Scituate—litigation rates failed to rise during the period 1797 to 1810 and, in fact, changed only slightly during the entire post-Revolutionary period. A fact common to the history of all three towns is that each declined in population between 1790 and 1800 and gained only enough new inhabitants between 1800 and 1810 to surpass slightly its 1790 total. Thus, overall growth between 1790 and 1810, the period in which intratown litigation was rising in the other towns, was marginal. Hanover gained only 87 inhabitants over the 20 years, Marshfield 95, and Scituate 113.

When intratown litigation totals for the three towns are aggregated in fifteen-year intervals, the totals, with one exception, always decline during the post-Revolutionary period. Table 4.5 presents the number of intratown cases in each town and the total number of cases in all three towns for each of the three periods.

Nor did litigation in Hanover, Marshfield, and Scituate become increasingly an activity of a small rising elite in the

TABLE 4.5 Three Towns: Frequency of Intratown Cases, 1781–1825

	Cases 1781–1795	*Cases 1796–1810*	*Cases 1811–1825*
Hanover	53	49	31
Marshfield	33	27	22
Scituate	92	90	114
Total	178	166	167

early years of the nineteenth century, as it did in every other town except Plymouth. In Hanover, 5 men who made 8 or more appearances, 2 of whom were manufacturers and 1 of whom was a house builder, made a total of 51 appearances in intratown cases between 1781 and 1825. They made 15 of those appearances between 1781 and 1795, 27 of them between 1796 and 1810, and 9 of them between 1811 and 1825. Likewise, the two men in Marshfield who made 8 or more appearances—merchant Calvin Lewis and yeoman Isaac Ford—made 11 of those appearances during 1781–95, 5 during 1796–1810, and 3 during 1811–25. Finally, in Scituate, where 14 men, including 4 merchants, 3 manufacturers, a deputy sheriff, a selectman, and 2 town meeting moderators, made 8 or more appearances, the total of 154 appearances between 1781 and 1825 was spread quite evenly. Forty-two occurred during 1781–95, and 56 occurred during each of the two later periods, 1796–1810 and 1811–25. When all three towns are examined in conjunction, it develops that appearances by litigious individuals peaked at 88 in the middle period, 1796–1810, rising from 68 in the earlier period, 1781–95, and falling again to 68 in the final period, 1811–25.

The only change in the litigation patterns of Hanover, Marshfield, and Scituate that paralleled changes in the other towns in the county was that litigation did tend to become increasingly commercial as the post-Revolutionary period advanced. Thus, in the first fifteen years after the Revolution, Hanover had 10 cases in which a commercial litigant appeared —19 percent of all cases. From 1796 to 1810, on the other hand, commercial litigants appeared in 46 percent of Hanover's intratown cases, while from 1811 to 1825 they appeared in 32 percent. Marshfield exhibited a similar pattern. Commercial cases rose from 16 percent of all intratown litigation during 1781–95 to 64 percent during 1796–1810 and further to 77 percent during 1811–25. Likewise, in Scituate, commercial litigation rose from 25 percent of all intratown cases during 1781–95 to 55 percent during 1796–1810, but then fell to 44 percent during 1811–25. Examined in conjunction, the three towns had 40 commercial cases, or 22 percent of their intratown total, during 1781–96; 88 cases, or 53 percent of their total, during 1796–1810; and 75 cases, or 45 percent of their total, during 1811–25.

But, despite this typical rise in commercial litigation, the central fact about the pattern of intratown litigation in Hanover, Marshfield, and Scituate is its remarkable stability throughout the entire forty-five years after the Revolution, a period during which litigation patterns elsewhere in the county were undergoing dramatic change. This stable pattern of intratown litigation seems best explained by the fact that the three towns in which it occurred were different from most of the rest of the towns in Plymouth County in that the commercial and industrial revolutions in large measure passed them by. In the language of one nineteenth-century historian of Scituate, the three towns were "not advancing greatly in business enterprise" and were never overwhelmed by "the haunts of trade."[53] As a result, their rate of growth was low and basic habits of life remained far more stable than in the rest of the county.

The General Increase in Intratown Litigation: A More Precise View

The town-by-town analysis of changing patterns of intratown litigation facilitates more precise analysis of the overall pattern of post-Revolutionary change. First, the analysis of the separate towns indicates that the period from 1787 to 1805, which had earlier appeared as a single span of rising intratown litigation, should be examined in two separate parts: the ten years prior to 1797 and the nine years from 1797 to 1805. During the first period, there was a total of 642 intratown cases in all fourteen towns, for an average of 64.20 cases per year—an intratown litigation rate lower than the pre-Revolutionary rate of 71.24 cases per year. Probably as a result of jurisdictional changes in 1787–88 that sought to discourage litigation in the Court of Common Pleas, the total number of cases, both intratown and intertown, instituted by county residents in that court declined even more sharply to 1,010—a rate of 101.00 cases per year compared to the pre-Revolutionary rate of 167.20 cases per year. Thus, intratown litigation, which had constituted 43 percent of the litigation total before the Revolution, rose to 64 percent of the total during the ten years beginning in 1787.

This change, the product of a sharp decline in the amount of recorded intertown litigation, is attributable in large part to the statistical influence of four towns. The most important of those was Plymouth, whose residents had commenced 31 percent of all intertown litigation in the county prior to the Revolution. Beginning in 1781, however, the amount of intertown litigation brought by Plymouth plaintiffs declined sharply to only 6 percent. The three other towns were those in the stagnant northeast—Hanover, Scituate, and Marshfield—whose residents had together commenced another 20 percent of pre-Revolutionary intertown litigation. After the Revolution, the three towns brought only 8 percent of the intertown cases. At the same time that intertown litigation declined sharply in the four towns, intratown litigation fell only slightly—from 32.08 cases per year during the half-century before the Revolution to 30.31 cases per year during 1787–1825. As a result of this disparity, litigation involving only residents of a single town, which before the Revolution had amounted to 40 percent of all litigation commenced by residents of the four towns, rose between 1787 and 1825 to 74 percent.

In the ten remaining towns, the pattern of change was different. Between 1787 and 1796, residents of these towns —Abington, Bridgewater, Duxbury, Halifax, Kingston, Middleboro, Pembroke, Plympton, Rochester, and Wareham— appeared as plaintiffs in 346 intratown and 436 intertown cases, a total of 782 cases in all. This yields an average of 34.60 intratown cases per year, a decline of between 4 and 5 cases per year from the pre-Revolutionary average of 39.16 cases. Intratown cases, which had constituted 46 percent of all litigation in the ten towns during the half century before the Revolution, fell to 44 percent between 1787 and 1796.

Then, in 1797, intratown and ultimately intracommunity litigation began a steep rise in the group of ten towns where rates for ten years had been nearly stable. In that year, the ten towns, which had been averaging 34.60 intratown cases per year, had a total of 65 intratown cases. This was followed by a total of 81 cases in 1798 and 72 in 1799, with a total of 575 cases between 1797 and 1805 and an average of 63.89 cases per year. During the same period, intertown litigation rose less rapidly to a total of 563 cases. As a result, intratown litigation rose from 44 percent of all cases instituted by plaintiffs in those towns to 51 percent. After 1806, intratown litigation continued to rise in the ten towns to a twenty-year total of 2,047 cases by 1825, or an average of 102.35 cases per year. During the same twenty-year period, the ten towns had 1,623 intertown cases. As a result, intratown litigation rose further to 56 percent of total litigation.

Accordingly, in the group of ten towns, intratown litigation during the years 1806–25 was significantly higher than it had been during the pre-Revolutionary period, both in the absolute number of cases and in the percentage of all litigation that was of an intratown nature. This rise in intratown litigation, moreover, does not fully reflect the rise that occurred in litigation among neighbors because it does not measure the increasing proportion of intratown litigation in Bridgewater and Middleboro and perhaps Rochester that was of an intracommunity nature. The rise in litigation among neighbors did not occur immediately after the Revolution, but began in the late 1790s, when intratown litigation began to constitute a higher percentage of all litigation, and continued into the first ten years of the nineteenth century.

In the remaining four towns in the county, litigation patterns underwent little change after 1797. In the three stagnant towns of the northeast—Hanover, Marshfield, and Scituate—post-Revolutionary patterns nearly duplicated pre-Revolutionary ones, except that residents of the three towns brought significantly fewer suits against residents of other towns in the county. In Plymouth, however, there was one other change that did make its litigation pattern more comparable to the patterns of the other ten towns after 1797: a sharp rise not in the total quantity of intratown cases but in the number of town residents participating in them.

As more residents of Plymouth began to take part in its unchanging rate of intratown litigation, several other towns in the county were developing litigation patterns in which a smaller number of litigants accounted for a larger percentage of their increasing number of cases. The result was that the litigation patterns of Plymouth and several of the other towns in the county, which were quite different prior to 1797, began to converge thereafter. Table 4.6 illustrates this phenomenon by comparing average annual rates of intracommunity litigation during 1787–96 and by then showing their convergence during 1811–25. The three stagnant northeast towns—Hanover, Marshfield, and Scituate—that exhibit a distinctive pattern throughout the post-Revolutionary period are omitted from the table. As table 4.6 shows, Plymouth, as before the Revolution, had a uniquely large rate of intracommunity litigation during the period 1787–96—about 6 times as high as that of Bridgewater, the next most litigious town, and 182 times as high as that of Halifax, the least litigious town. From 1811 to 1825, on the other hand, Plymouth was no longer the most litigious town in the county. Bridgewater, the most litigious, had 2.15 cases per year more than Plymouth. Those two towns, moreover, no longer stood dramatically ahead of the county's other towns. The third most litigious, Middleboro, had 63 percent as much litigation as Bridgewater, and Bridgewater had only about fifteen times as much litigation as Halifax, the least litigious town. When the averages are ad-

TABLE 4.6 Eleven Towns: Frequency of Intracommunity Cases, 1787–1825[54]

	Cases per Year 1787–1796	*Cases per 1,000 Residents 1787–1796*	*Cases per Year 1811–1825*	*Cases per 1,000 Residents 1811–1825*
Plymouth	18.20	6.08	19.93	4.58
Bridgewater[55]	3.10	0.62	22.08	3.89
Duxbury	2.90	1.99	5.47	2.28
Pembroke	2.60	1.33	8.33	3.76
Plympton	2.90	1.61	6.13	3.47
Middleboro[56]	2.42	0.53	13.80	2.94
Rochester[57]	2.12	0.80	6.87	2.26
Kingston	1.60	1.59	3.53	2.69
Abington	0.30	0.21	6.87	3.58
Wareham	0.30	0.35	2.53	2.66
Halifax	0.10	0.15	1.47	1.96

justed by population, it appears that Plymouth, which in 1790 had more than 3 times the rate of intratown litigation of Duxbury, the second most litigious town, had only 1.2 times as much litigation per capita as Pembroke, the second most litigious town in 1820. The table also shows that Plymouth in 1790 had 41 times as much litigation per capita as Halifax, the least litigious town, whereas it had only 2.3 times as much as Halifax, still the least litigious town in 1820. Finally, the table shows that, although the number of intratown cases per 1,000 residents declined in Plymouth between 1790 and 1820, it rose in every other one of the towns listed in the table.

Until 1797, Plymouth differed from the rest of the towns in the county in that most of its intratown litigation was brought by a small group of litigious individuals who appeared in court at least 8 or more times during their careers. This was not true in any other town. Table 4.7 presents data for all towns except the three stagnant northeast ones as to the total number of appearances made by all litigants from 1781 to 1797, the number of appearances by litigious persons, the number of appearances by nonlitigious ones and the percentage of total appearances by the litigious. As table 4.7 shows, Plymouth prior to 1797 again had a statistical pattern quite distinct from the patterns of the other towns.

Table 4.8 calculates the average number of appearances per year by nonlitigious people in each town prior to 1797 and the number of appearances per 1,000 inhabitants on the basis of the census of 1790. As table 4.8 shows, the number of appearances by nonlitigious individuals in Plymouth's intratown litigation was not strikingly larger than the number of appearances by such people in the other towns if the number is adjusted by population. Thus, as has already been seen, what differentiated litigation patterns in Plymouth from those in the other towns prior to 1797 was the fact that Plymouth

TABLE 4.7 Eleven Towns: Frequency of Appearances by Litigious and Nonlitigious Residents, 1781–1797

	Total Cases	*By Litigious Residents*	*By Nonlitigious Residents*	*Percent of Total by Litigious Residents*
Plymouth[58]	797	464	333	58.2%
Bridgewater	612	134	478	21.9%
Middleboro	488	102	386	20.9%
Duxbury	123	21	102	17.1%
Plympton	143	23	120	16.1%
Rochester	256	41	215	16.0%
Pembroke	130	18	112	13.8%
Kingston	57	6	49	10.5%
Abington	41	0	41	0.0%
Wareham	33	0	33	0.0%
Halifax	18	0	18	0.0%

contained a small group of commercially oriented litigants unlike any similar group in any other town.

Beginning in 1797, this difference disappeared. Table 4.9 presents data comparable to that of table 4.7, for the period 1798–1825. Table 4.10 gives data comparable to that in table 4.8, also for the period 1798–1825, on the basis of the 1820 census.

As table 4.9 shows, Plymouth after 1797 no longer stood out above the other towns with an unusually large percentage of its litigation brought by a small group of litigious individuals. Indeed, the percentage of cases brought by such litigants declined in Plymouth, while it simultaneously rose in every other town except Duxbury. As a result, Plymouth fell from first to second place in table 4.9. In this table, unlike table

TABLE 4.8 Eleven Towns: Frequency of Appearances by Nonlitigious Residents, 1781–1797

	By Nonlitigious Residents per Year	*Cases per 1,000 Inhabitants*
Plymouth	20.81	6.95
Bridgewater	28.12	5.65
Middleboro	22.71	5.02
Rochester	12.65	4.78
Duxbury	6.00	4.13
Plympton	7.06	3.92
Pembroke	6.59	3.37
Kingston	2.88	2.87
Wareham	1.94	2.27
Abington	2.41	1.66
Halifax	1.06	1.60

4.7, no clear breaks mark off those towns in which a few people participated in a large portion of the intratown litigation from those towns in which the litigation was more widespread.

A comparison of table 4.10 with table 4.8 shows that the number of appearances per year by nonlitigious individuals, adjusted by population, did not change sharply between the period before and the period after 1797. In most towns, the number of appearances rose by one or two per year—a reflection of the general increase in intratown litigation, although in three towns, Plymouth,[59] Duxbury, and Kingston, the number fell. More striking is the difference in the average annual number of appearances per 1,000 inhabitants made by highly litigious individuals. These figures, based on the 1790 and 1820 censuses, are presented in table 4.11 for the pre-1797

TABLE 4.9 Eleven Towns: Frequency of Appearances by Litigious and Nonlitigious Residents, 1798–1825

	Total Cases	*By Litigious Residents*	*By Nonlitigious Residents*	*Percent of Total by Litigious Residents*
Middleboro	1,888	918	970	48.6%
Plymouth[60]	1,298	570	728	43.9%
Plympton	443	171	272	38.6%
Bridgewater	1,442	481	961	33.4%
Rochester	814	229	585	28.1%
Abington	316	81	235	25.6%
Kingston	117	26	91	22.2%
Pembroke	417	72	345	17.3%
Duxbury	304	47	257	15.5%
Wareham	126	14	112	11.1%
Halifax	81	8	73	9.9%

and post-1798 periods. Table 4.11 demonstrates that the amount of litigation involving the highly litigious dropped sharply in Plymouth from an unusually high figure to an amount that placed Plymouth only second in the county. The table also shows a slight drop in the figures for Duxbury. Finally, the table indicates a rise in all the other towns in the annual number of cases involving the highly litigious—sometimes as much as a fivefold rise in a town like Middleboro or a rise from no cases to a substantial number in a town like Abington. In other words, table 4.11 shows again the statistical patterns of Plymouth and the other towns converging.

The pattern of statistical change in post-Revolutionary intratown litigation can now be summarized. In the first fifteen years that the courts were open to hear substantial numbers

TABLE 4.10 Eleven Towns: Frequency of Appearances by Nonlitigious Residents, 1798–1825

	By Nonlitigious Residents per Year	*Cases per 1,000 Inhabitants*
Middleboro	34.64	7.39
Rochester	20.89	6.89
Bridgewater	34.32	6.05
Plymouth	25.10	5.77
Pembroke	12.32	5.56
Plympton	9.71	5.49
Abington	8.39	4.37
Wareham	4.00	4.20
Duxbury	9.18	3.82
Halifax	2.61	3.48
Kingston	3.25	2.48

of cases, 1781 to 1795, pre-Revolutionary patterns tended to persist. That meant that in all the towns, except Plymouth, intracommunity litigation remained at or near its low pre-Revolutionary rate, with few commercial litigants appearing in the cases and few litigants of any sort appearing in court with great frequency. In Plymouth, the pre-Revolutionary pattern also continued. A small number of highly litigious, commercial individuals appeared frequently before the courts, while the remainder of the town's residents, like their counterparts in the county's other towns, sued each other only rarely. By the period 1811–25, however, a new, nineteenth-century pattern that was relatively uniform throughout eleven towns had emerged. In the new pattern, every town had a rate of intracommunity litigation among nonlitigious persons that

TABLE 4.11 Eleven Towns: Frequency of Appearances by Highly Litigious Residents, 1781–1825

	Annual Appearances 1781–1797	*Annual Appearances 1798–1825*
Middleboro	1.33	7.00
Plymouth	9.11	4.68
Plympton	0.75	3.45
Bridgewater	1.58	3.03
Rochester	0.91	2.70
Abington	0.00	1.51
Pembroke	0.54	1.16
Kingston	0.35	0.71
Duxbury	0.85	0.70
Wareham	0.00	0.53
Halifax	0.00	0.38

was higher than the low rates typical of the pre-Revolutionary era. Finally, every town had its highly litigious residents, who accounted for a substantial percentage of its litigation, although nowhere as much as in Plymouth before and immediately after the Revolution.

Of course, the extent to which each town conformed to this new nineteenth-century pattern, which in its essentials was the pattern that litigation had taken in the town of Plymouth in the eighteenth century, differed. There were also differences in the types of changes that took place in each of the towns as the old pattern was transformed into the new. There were, finally, differences in the precise timing of various changes, although the earliest time at which change began was the

1790s and the changes appear to have been completed by 1810—not an exceptionally long period of time.

In any event, one central fact is clear: between the 1780s and 1810, ten towns in Plymouth County—Abington, Bridgewater, Duxbury, Halifax, Kingston, Middleboro, Pembroke, Plympton, Rochester, and Wareham—ceased to adhere to the statistical pattern of intratown litigation which they had evidenced throughout most of the eighteenth century. Instead, they assumed the pattern that, in its essentials, had been prevalent during the eighteenth century only in the town of Plymouth. Three towns alone remained loyal to their old ways. In short, a special, local, and minority pattern of dispute resolution became the dominant one. Why?

5 Commerce, Religion, Politics, and the Nineteenth-Century Increase in Litigation

Chapter 3 pointed out that the existence of religious division or the presence of commercially oriented residents in a town seemed to have an impact on the rate of intracommunity litigation. If at least one of those factors was present, a high litigation rate would be experienced; if both were absent, the rate of intracommunity litigation would tend to remain low. Chapter 4 indicated that most towns took on highly litigious patterns in the post-Revolutionary period. Were the same two factors that led disputants to take their cases to court in pre-Revolutionary Plymouth County still operating after the Revolution? First, the impact of commerce will be analyzed.

Commerce

There can be no doubt that much of the increased litigation in the post-Revolutionary period was commercial in character. Indeed, in every town in the county except Halifax, intratown litigation involving at least one commercial party grew more rapidly than intratown litigation in general. Accordingly, commercial litigation came to constitute a higher percentage of each town's litigation during the period 1811–25 for the prerise period in each town, and the 1820 census is used for the postrise period.

Table 5.3 shows that three towns in the county—Duxbury, Kingston, and Plymouth—experienced only slight increases in their rate of noncommercial litigation once population increases are taken into account. Thus, Duxbury's litigation rate increased by only 21 percent, or .10 cases per year; Kingston's by only 20 percent, or .16 cases per year; and Plymouth's by 30 percent, or .13 cases per year. In every other town listed in the table, noncommercial litigation more than doubled at the time of the litigation rise.

In short, when commercial litigation is subtracted from the intracommunity totals, a pattern emerges in which there is either no rise or only a slight rise in noncommercial litigation in three towns—Duxbury, Kingston, and Plymouth—during the post-Revolutionary period. In addition, as has already been seen, three other towns—Hanover, Marshfield, and Scituate—experienced declines in their rates of noncommercial litigation. It is worth noting that five of these six towns are the only ones in the county lying on the county's eastern, or Atlantic, shore. Furthermore, the sixth—Hanover—is contiguous to Scituate, has both northern and eastern borders that are only six miles from the sea, and throughout both the nineteenth and twentieth centuries has had a character more like that of coastal towns, to the east, than that of the inland towns, to the west.[13] In the northerly three of these towns—Hanover, Marshfield, and Scituate—where the early nineteenth century brought little new commercial and industrial activity and little population growth, total intracommunity litigation either failed to rise or declined. In the southerly three of the towns—Duxbury, Kingston, and Plymouth—where commercial and industrial activity and population rose dramatically, total intracommunity litigation did rise. Nearly

than it had during the period 1781–95. Table 5.1 presents the data on the changing percentages. Table 5.1 leaves little doubt that the spread of commerce must have contributed significantly to the increase in intracommunity litigation in post-Revolutionary Plymouth County. However, as will now be shown, the rise in commercial litigation can account for only a part and not the whole of the turn-of-the century rise in intracommunity lawsuits.

Because we know both the average number of intracommunity cases per year[1] and the percentage of those cases that were of a commercial character,[2] we can estimate the average number of noncommercial intracommunity cases per year for each town. Table 5.2 gives this information for the period

TABLE 5.1 Fourteen Towns: Percentage of Commercial Litigation, 1781–1795 and 1811–1825

	1781–1795	*1811–1825*
Abington	3.8%	45.1%
Bridgewater	16.1%	29.4%
Duxbury	70.5%	82.5%
Halifax	20.0%	4.5%
Hanover	19.2%	32.3%
Kingston	20.9%	69.2%
Marshfield	16.1%	77.3%
Middleboro	10.9%	32.7%
Pembroke	22.9%	42.1%
Plymouth	47.4%	75.3%
Plympton	8.3%	45.0%
Rochester	32.3%	38.8%
Scituate	25.3%	44.4%
Wareham	20.0%	24.3%

before and the period after the rise in litigation began in each of ten towns in which the number of intracommunity cases rose. As Table 5.2 shows, every town listed experienced a substantial increase in its noncommercial, intracommunity litigation beginning sometime between 1797 and 1806. It should also be noted that the town of Plymouth, which experienced a litigation rise only in the form of increased citizen participation in lawsuits, witnessed an increase in the number of such suits not involving commercial litigants. Until 1797, Plymouth had had an average of 2.50 cases per year in which no litigious citizens had appeared;[3] because 48 percent of all of the town's cases during this period involved a litigant engaged in either commerce or manufacturing, an estimate can be made that Plymouth had an average of 1.30 noncommercial cases not involving litigious citizens. Beginning in 1797, on the other hand, it had 7.83 cases per year in which the

TABLE 5.2 Ten Towns: Estimated Number of Noncommercial Intracommunity Cases before and after Rise in Litigation

	Cases before Rise	*Cases after Rise*
Middleboro[4]	2.15	8.81
Bridgewater[5]	2.62	15.59
Rochester[6]	1.70	4.16
Abington[7]	0.64	3.38
Duxbury[7]	0.68	1.38
Halifax[8]	0.25	1.57
Kingston[9]	0.80	1.26
Pembroke[8]	1.92	5.12
Plympton[8]	2.34	4.84
Wareham[10]	0.24	1.36

litigious were not involved;[11] 69 percent of these were mercial in the above sense, which leaves a total of 2.43 per year that were noncommercial. This represents, of c a substantial rise from the 1.30 average for the pre period.

It may be, however, that in at least some towns the noncommercial intracommunity litigation merely mirr approximately equal increase in population. Table 5.3 the data given in table 5.2 and the data given above fo outh, so that the average number of cases is restate average number per 1,000 residents for prerise and periods. The 1790 census is used to supply populatio

TABLE 5.3 Ten Towns Plus Plymouth: Estimated Number of Noncommercial Intracommunity Cases before and after Rise in Litigation[12]

	Cases per 1,000 Residents before Rise	*Cases per 1,000 Residents after Rise*
Middleboro	0.48	1.88
Bridgewater	0.53	2.75
Rochester	0.64	1.37
Abington	0.44	1.76
Duxbury	0.47	0.57
Halifax	0.38	2.10
Kingston	0.80	0.96
Pembroke	0.98	2.31
Plympton	1.30	2.74
Wareham	0.28	1.43
Plymouth	0.43	0.56

all of this increase in litigation may be attributable directly to the rise in commerce, industry, and population. And even the small portion of the litigation rise that cannot be directly attributed to these three factors can, perhaps, be indirectly attributed on the theory that, as nonlitigious, agrarian people saw increasingly large numbers of their commercial and industrial neighbors taking their disputes to court, they began to do the same.

Thus, it may be that commerce, industry, and population growth were the only factors contributing to the early nineteenth-century breakdown of nonjudicial patterns of dispute resolution in the towns of Plymouth County lying on or near the eastern shore. However, in the county's six remaining inland towns—Abington, Bridgewater, Halifax, Middleboro, Pembroke, and Plympton—and in the two south shore towns of Rochester and Wareham, other forces were almost surely at work. In all these towns there was a substantial rise in litigation that cannot be attributed directly to the growth of commerce, industry, and population. Moreover, although the litigation patterns of pre-Revolutionary Plymouth and of post-Revolutionary Duxbury, Kingston, and Plymouth suggest that increases in commercial litigation may produce secondary increases in agrarian litigation as nonlitigious farmers begin to copy the litigious habits of their commercial neighbors, these same patterns also suggest that, if such secondary increases occur at all, they are small. Thus, it appears that factors other than commerce must have contributed to the breakdown of informal eighteenth-century methods of dispute resolution and hence to the nineteenth-century litigation rise.

Religion

This study has indicated that on a number of occasions during the pre-Revolutionary period religious conflict and division within a community produced a sharp rise in the amount of litigation between neighbors in that community. Given the importance of the local congregation as an instrument for the resolution of private disputes, this fact is not at all surprising. Might religious conflict similarly have contributed to the breakdown of nonjudicial devices for dispute resolution in the late eighteenth and early nineteenth centuries? The answer is that it probably did, for every town in the interior of the county experienced significant religious dissent and upheaval in the half-century following the Revolution.

In Middleboro, it will be recalled, three separate Baptist congregations had been founded prior to the Revolution—in Titicut, Rock Village, and Lakeville. After the Revolution, it seems clear that these congregations each grew in size and probably in importance.[14] It appears that Baptists, who prior to the Revolution had played an insignificant role in the town's life and had rarely appeared in litigation, began to enter the mainstream of town activity. Indeed, three of them—William Nelson, Levi Peirce, and Samuel Pickens—held a variety of key offices. Pickens, the first to be elected, served as a selectman from 1799 to 1801 and again from 1804 to 1816; as representative to the General Court from 1807 to 1810 and again in 1816; and as a justice of the peace after 1808. The next Baptist voted into office was Peirce. In 1805, he was chosen both town treasurer, a position he held for two terms, and representative to the General Court, where he sat for six years, and in 1819 was named a justice of the peace. Nelson became a selectman in 1814, a position he held until 1819, and a justice of the peace in 1824.[15]

At the same time, Baptists[16] began to appear with greater frequency in the courts. Although they had appeared in only 19 Middleboro intratown cases prior to the Revolution and in only 17 cases between 1781 and 1795, they took part in at least 113 cases during the three decades beginning in 1796, or 13 percent of Middleboro's total. These numbers, it should be noted, understate Baptist appearances in litigation because the members of the Second Baptist Church of Middleboro, whose records have been lost,[17] were not included in the tally. A final piece of evidence of the growing centrality of the Baptist denomination in the life of the town is that, whereas the denomination's adherents had consistently lived on the outskirts before the Revolution, they began to move into the town center thereafter. The culmination of this movement occurred in 1828, when the Central Baptist Church was founded.[18] The growing importance of this evangelical sect, whose doctrine and membership often refused to accord respect to traditional figures of authority, could well have produced a destabilizing effect on Middleboro's inherited patterns of dispute resolution, particularly in conjunction with the growth of commerce in the town.

As in Middleboro, Baptist congregations had met in Bridgewater, in both the Titicut and West parishes, in the eighteenth century.[19] An Anglican church had also been founded in the town in 1747; it was revived in 1816.[20] During the post-Revolutionary period, new dissensions appeared. A historian of North Bridgewater notes, for example, that an "unhappy division" existed in that town's church in the years immediately preceding 1810 that ultimately resulted in the firing of the church's minister in 1811. His successor was apparently more acceptable to the majority of the congregation, and in 1816 he was able to bring about an evangelical revival in the town.[21] He was less satisfactory, however, to the minority, which seceded from the church in 1824 to form a new congregation that espoused more liberal religious views.[22] A similar split between Trinitarians and Unitarians was emerging in both Bridgewater Center and East Bridgewater in the first two decades of the nineteenth century, culminating in the secession of Trinitarians from the two congregations, in 1821 in Bridgewater Center and in 1826 in East Bridgewater.[23] Meanwhile, members of the Swedenborgian Church had founded congregations in the Bridgewaters—in 1820 in North Bridgewater and in 1824 in Bridgewater Center.[24] Thus, by the 1820s the Bridgewaters were witness to a religious cacophony of Episcopalians, Unitarians, Congregationalists, Baptists, and Swedenborgians. Unfortunately, too many church records have been lost in the town to make it possible to specify the statistical impact of this dissension on intracommunity litigation.

In the smaller inland towns, the pattern of dissension was less complicated, but not inherently different. In Pembroke, a schism in the West Parish between Unitarians and Congregationalists began as early as 1803, when a woman in the church prayed for the "Lord [to] change" the minister's "heart, or take him from the ministry;"[25] in 1826, the Unitarians apparently left the church.[26] Meanwhile, in 1811, a Baptist church had been founded in Pembroke.[27] In neighboring Abington, the church records for 1804 note "difficulties subsisting in this place respecting singing in public worship"—difficulties which disrupted "that peace and harmony which ought to subsist in every religious society."[28] These difficulties were resolved in 1806,[29] but new problems soon arose when the Congregationalist minister began preaching Swedenborgian doctrines; although he was fired and forced to leave town in 1821, his followers remained and in 1827 organized a new church of their own.[30]

To the south, in Halifax, a Baptist church had been established by 1821,[31] and farther to the south, in Carver, a Baptist church had been founded somewhat earlier, in 1791.[32] Meanwhile, in neighboring Wareham, a Methodist church had been established in 1812.[33] Finally, in the south shore town of Rochester, some members of the Congregational church in the North Parish joined a nearby Baptist church in Middleboro in the early years of the nineteenth century,[34] and Baptists elsewhere in the town joined together sometime before 1805 to organize the United Baptist Church. Baptists from the latter church,[35] together with Quakers who continued to reside in Rochester,[36] appeared in 57 cases in Rochester, or 16 percent of the town's total, over the period 1803–25—a sharp increase from the period 1781–1802, when the two groups had appeared in only 11 cases, or 8 percent of the total.

Similar religious dissent prevailed in Plymouth and Kingston and may have accounted for that portion of the rise in intratown litigation in those two towns that cannot be explained as the direct product of increasing commerce and manufacturing. In Plymouth, the Trinitarians seceded from the increasingly Unitarian First Church in 1802–3, a Baptist church was founded in 1809, and a Univeralist church appeared in 1822.[37] In Kingston, the Baptists established a congregation in 1804.[38]

The establishment of Baptist churches in Marshfield in 1788[39] and Hanover in 1806[40] may even have had a temporary destabilizing effect in those towns. Fully 33 of Hanover's 133 post-Revolutionary intratown cases took place during the four years immediately preceding 1806, and 15 of Marshfield's total of 82 cases occurred during the three years leading up to the founding of its Baptist church; another 15 of Marshfield's cases took place during the five-year period 1809–13, at the end of which a Methodist church was established in the town.[41] Only in Scituate, where the sole new dissenting church established between the Revolution and the mid-1820s was of the noncontentious Universalist denomination,[42] does there appear to have been no rise in intracommunity litigation that can possibly be ascribed to growing religious dissent.

What emerges, finally, from a comparison of post-Revolutionary and pre-Revolutionary intracommunity litigation is a pattern similar to that which emerged from comparison of the litigious and nonlitigious towns during the pre-Revolutionary period. Both before and after the Revolution, disputes involving either parties with religious differences or parties engaged in commercial occupations appear to have been beyond the competence of institutions like the church and thus necessitated judicial intervention. At least during the pre-Revolutionary period, when neither commerce nor religious division was widespread in Plymouth County, it further appears that either of these phenomena was a force capable by itself of disrupting communitarian processes of dispute resolution. Thus, the presence of commercial litigants in the town of Plymouth during the half-century before the Revolution gave it an unusually high rate of intratown litigation throughout the period, during a large portion of which it exhibited no significant religious divisions.

On the other hand, in towns like Pembroke and Middleboro, where few residents earned their living through commerce, the presence of religious division, either in the form of a dissenting sect like the Quakers or in the form of a church schism, brought many cases to court at least while the division was at its height. It also appears from analysis of the post-Revolutionary period, when both religious division and commerce were widespread, that the two forces were capable of operating in conjunction to bring most communitarian dispute-resolution efforts to a halt and compel disputants to take their cases to court. Post-Revolutionary Bridgewater and Middleboro, which experienced substantial increases in the size of their commercial populations, in the extent of their religious divisions, and in their rate of intracommunity litigation, best illustrate how the two forces of commerce and religious division may have worked together to bring about litigation increases that neither force alone could have produced.

Politics

The expansion of commerce and the spread of religious dissent may not, however, have been the only changes in the years around 1800 to which the early nineteenth century rise in litigation related. It may also have been associated with another contemporaneous development: the institutionalization of partisan political conflict.

Except during the Great Awakening, which, as has been seen, led to temporary religious divisions in a few Plymouth towns, sustained county-wide division probably did not occur before 1765. During the next fifteen years, however, the "public affairs of this Province"[43] required frequent and continual attention from local bodies politic. During that decade and a half, town meetings were continually voting upon such matters as how best to preserve liberty,[44] whether to declare independence,[45] how to procure and support soldiers,[46] and whether to ratify a state constitution.[47] Although town clerks almost always recorded votes as being taken "unanimously"[48] during the decade between the Stamp Act and the decision for independence, the unanimity they observed may have been more for the purpose of impressing the British authorities than a reflection of the actual state of affairs in most towns.

One piece of evidence comes out of Plymouth, where the town meeting on December 7, 1773—nine days before the Boston Tea Party—voted unanimously to support Boston in its opposition to the landing of the tea, and then on December 13—three days before the Tea Party—was confronted with a motion to reconsider that vote. The vote on the motion to reconsider—20 in favor and 52 against—suggests that the town was less than truly unanimous in its revolutionary fervor.[49] Any breakdown that may have occurred in political unanimity did not, however, lead to an immediate breakdown of the process of dispute resolution, if for no other reason than the self-interest of the Tory minority in the continued functioning of those processes.

During the years of the War for Independence, on the other hand, town clerks in Plymouth County abandoned the pretense that decisions were taken unanimously. In Middleboro, for example, a town meeting in September 1777, by a majority of nine votes, reversed an earlier decision that one William Canady was "inimical" to American interests. A recount demanded by "a Number of Persons . . . [who] Did not understand" the thrust of the motion on which they had just voted produced further discord when "a Number of Persons . . . Pretended to vote that Were not Voters," and in the end the town meeting had to be adjourned,[50] for the issue of identifying and punishing Tories had shattered Middleboro's unanimity. Unanimity similarly collapsed over the issue of supporting the army. In Plymouth, the necessary taxation was approved on a close 22–16 vote,[51] while in Marshfield the issue led to "great uneasiness and warm debates" that culminated in a meeting at which proxy votes were received and a final vote was taken.[52] Throughout the county, votes on the proposed constitution of 1778 and on the constitution adopted in 1780 were rarely taken with unanimity.[53] In fact, the only issue relating to war and independence on which the towns were said to have preserved their unanimity was the necessity for regulating prices and thereby restraining inflation.[54]

Of course, the war years were aberrational ones in the history of Massachusetts. During this era, economic and sometimes social relationships were unhinged, the courts in large part ceased to function, and disputes lay unresolved.[55] After independence had been attained, however, political practice in the towns gave the appearance of reverting to normal, as did the process of dispute resolution. Town meeting adjudications of fence disputes again became common,[56] and meetings again began considering the utility of mills[57] and passing upon the rights of individuals who were using town lands or owed a debt to a town.[58] Although the failure of town clerks to record whether most votes were taken unanimously or upon a division makes it impossible to speak with statistical precision, it does not appear that town decisions were less unanimous during the 1780s than they had been during the half-century before the Revolution.[59] More significantly, it is clear that, once the constitution of 1780 had been ratified, high politics ceased for more than a decade to intrude into the still insular public life of Plymouth County towns.

In the mid-1790s, however, national and state affairs again began to intrude into local politics. In 1796, for example, a town meeting in Bridgewater, at which more than four hundred voters were present, declared "by a large and respectable majority" that Jay's Treaty should be put into effect,[60] and in the same year the town of Carver "[v]oted Unanimously" that a memorial should "be Transmitted to our Representative in Congress."[61] Twelve years later, the residents of Scituate voted "almost unanimously" to send a petition to President

Jefferson requesting repeal of the 1807 embargo,[62] as did also the town of Duxbury.[63] Four years later, Duxbury voted that its resolutions concerning "the impolitick and Ruinous effects of the present war" should be published in Boston newspapers and that its delegates to a county convention should "Circulate a memorial for peace & . . . procure as many signers as possible."[64] In 1814, the voters of Hanover expressed their "unqualified disapprobation" of a resolution in support of President Madison.[65] Votes of this sort almost surely resulted in local political controversy: Madison's supporters, for example, must have sensed some chance of victory when they brought their petition forward in the town meeting, while even in the seaport of Scituate, a few Jeffersonians opposed the town's petition for repeal of the 1807 embargo.

Partisan politics also exerted an impact on town electoral processes. In Hanover, for example, an eleven-man majority voted to send a representative to the General Court in 1808, but then proved unable to agree upon whom to send. After several ballots, the town reaffirmed its decision to send a representative by a fourteen-vote majority, but several more ballots were needed before a Jeffersonian Republican was finally elected to the office.[66]

An even more important development was the institutionalization of party divisions in gubernatorial elections in nearly every town in the county in the closing years of the eighteenth and the opening years of the nineteenth century. In 1795, before party divisions had come to Plymouth County, John Hancock, a nominal Republican, had carried every town. He garnered 95 percent or more of the vote in seven towns, between 90 and 95 percent in three towns, between 85 and 90 percent in two towns, 82 percent in one, and 76 percent in another. In Duxbury, the only town in which a close division occurred, Hancock carried 56 percent of the votes. During the decade 1801–10, on the other hand, only two towns remained heavily Republican: The party carried every gubernatorial election in Hanover with at least 81 percent of the vote and every election in Halifax with at least 83 percent. But political divisions came to every other town.

In Kingston and Plymouth, the Federalists won every gubernatorial race during the 1801–10 decade, but they received as little as 60 percent of the vote in Kingston and 57 percent in Plymouth. In Abington, Bridgewater, Middleboro, and Pembroke, the Republicans won all the elections except that of 1803. In Abington, their margin of victory ranged from 53 to 67 percent; in Middleboro, 57 to 70 percent; and in Pembroke, 51 to 71 percent. In Bridgewater, the Republicans captured 60 percent of the vote in 1801, but they never obtained more than 54 percent thereafter. In Scituate, the Republicans won seven out of ten elections, but they never received more than 58 percent of the vote. In five towns—Duxbury, Marshfield, Plympton, Rochester, and Wareham—no party won more than six out of the ten elections for governor. Finally, in Carver, where competitive politics did not arrive until 1806, Federalists carried three out of the five elections between that date and 1810, but never with more than 53 percent of the vote.[67]

Unfortunately, it is not possible to analyze the relationship between political conflict and the rate of litigation with the same precision with which the litigation rate could be related to commercial growth or even to the spread of religious dissent. It may be that no direct relationship existed between the institutionalization of partisan conflict and the early nineteenth-century increase in litigation. Both may have been products, entirely independently of each other, of the spread of commerce and religious dissent. On the other hand, the growing litigiousness of the early nineteenth century and the almost simultaneous appearance of modern party politics may have been related. Conclusions about a possible relation must, in the end, depend upon an understanding of the nature of eighteenth-century Plymouth society.

6 The Nature and the End of Community

This is an appropriate point to return to questions posed at the outset of this book concerning the character of New England towns. Substantial evidence has been presented indicating that, during the period 1725–74, thirteen out of Plymouth County's fourteen towns were insular communities at least insofar as they succeeded at most times in containing within their own borders conflicts and disputes that arose among their residents. These thirteen towns, moreover, were able to contain and resolve conflict without resorting to formal, legal instruments of physical coercion. The towns lacked an army or professional police force on which to call. The institutions on which they might have called—the militia and the local constabulary—possessed little more actual physical power than anyone whom they might have been asked to subdue, and would often have been unwilling to shoot at neighbors. Hence, these institutions were not called upon for law-enforcement purposes.[1] Communities were compelled to deal with conflicts and disputes by making use of means, other than force, that were at their disposal.

The means were a set of shared assumptions about how "good" people lived. These assumptions were prescribed at the level of moral ideal by church doctrine and confirmed at the level of practice by geographic, demographic, and technological realities that precluded most people from adopting styles of life radically different from the one they knew. The assumptions were enforced against recalcitrants on a day-to-day basis by sanctions ranging in severity from neighborly criticism to the ultimate sanction of ostracism.

Unfortunately I cannot prove by direct evidence that the functioning of the dispute-resolution process was related in eighteenth-century towns to such an insularity of values. Nor can direct evidence prove my belief that eighteenth-century Plymouth County communities were cohesive, insular entities whose inhabitants lived similar lives and abided by similar ethical values. This is the very point at issue among historians. What I can show is that, when competing value systems and other sorts of divisions imported from the outside world spread across Plymouth County during the 1790s and early 1800s, the system of internal resolution of disputes within communities collapsed. I can also show that earlier partial lapses in the system took place when similar divisive forces appeared in Plymouth locally or temporarily. On the basis of this evidence, I am prepared to infer that Plymouth's system of communitarian dispute resolution was not capable of functioning in the presence of significant social divisions. And, because the system did function effectively in most towns throughout most of the eighteenth century, I am further prepared to conclude that few serious social divisions endured during that century for any lengthy period of time.

If a dispute-resolution process such as that hypothesized in this book existed in eighteenth-century Plymouth County, the intrusion of national political issues into local life and the institutionalization of partisan strife surely must have helped to undermine it. If eighteenth-century localities resolved disputes and contained conflict by appealing to a consensus maintained in isolation from outside issues and ideas, the rise of national political organizations could not have been without some effect. National political coalitions intentionally bring outside issues to the attention of local electorates and bind local leaders into alliances with fellow partisans in other places instead of with their fellow townsmen. To the extent that political issues possess substantive social significance, party contests can have a deeply divisive impact on local communities. I believe that the rise of the first American party system exerted such an impact because it dissolved traditional relationships among people residing in the same locality and drove them into new alliances with like-minded people from other places.

The impact of institutionalized party conflict was, however, less significant than the contemporaneous breakdown of Plymouth County's ancient religious order. During the period around 1800 when political divisions were becoming the norm in Plymouth County, religious differences were also intensifying. Indeed, party conflict grew in part out of religious divisions, and a strong correlation existed between membership in a dissenting church and membership in the Jeffersonian party.[2] Chapter 5 demonstrated that religious dissent was increasing around 1800 in most towns throughout the county. It now remains necessary to show how the appearance of new religious ideas, often imported from the outside world, contributed to the breakdown, even in local life, of whatever unanimity remained in Plymouth towns as the eighteenth century ended and the nineteenth began.

The religious difficulties that plagued one of those towns, Plympton, were not different in kind from those that had arisen in pre-Revolutionary towns, especially during the Great Awakening. But they endured for a longer time because the town proved unable to imitate the pre-Revolutionary practice of restoring unanimity through compromise. The difficulties began in 1797, when the town was in need of a new minister. Of the three candidates, Ebenezer Withington received forty-eight votes; William Briggs, twenty-eight; and Abiel Williams, three. However, when the above "votes was [*sic*] disputed & the inhabitants were polled," Withington received fifty-two and Briggs twenty votes. The town then decided to "vote again to see if any more will fall in with the number that are in favor of" Withington, but the final count was only 56–17.[3] Withington was thereafter ordained, but he soon found himself in trouble when the town in 1800 voted 31–33 not to build a residence for him and 28–34 not to buy an existing house.[4] The next year, the ministry was offered to and accepted by John Briggs, but six years later the town balloted 20–45 not to permit him to buy or use the town's parsonage. That same year, Briggs's request for a dismission was granted.[5]

In 1808, Plympton voted 34–45 not to concur in the church's first choice of a man for the ministry,[6] but later in the year it concurred, 35–18, in the choice of Elijah Dexter.[7] The town then became embroiled in a dispute about which neighboring ministers should be invited to attend his ordination and who should preach the sermon—a dispute that undoubtedly carried theological overtones and reflected the town's awareness of the growing influence of outside religious ideas. After the town had voted 38–26 to accept a report of the committee charged with planning the ordination, seven voters moved for reconsideration and their motion was defeated by only eleven votes, 30–41.[8] Despite the controversy surrounding his ordination, Dexter succeeded for a decade in raising little controversy until in 1820 he sought a salary increase. By a vote of 90–0, twelve voters abstaining, the town agreed to pay him $400 instead of $350 per year,[9] but three years later a dispute arose over whether to appropriate the money from town funds. A vote by a show of hands indicated a one-vote majority for making the appropriation, but that vote was disputed; a second hand vote revealed that a majority opposed the appropriation. The town then voted by ballot, 38–60, not to appropriate the funds. The town clerk noted that "there was a shameful and disgraceful scene of confusion and disorder . . . in the Meeting, and the Moderator could not preserve order." Moreover, on the final vote, "10 persons voted who had Certificates recorded of membership in other religious societies, and did not belong to the town in its parochial capacity."[10] For a month, Plympton was without a salaried minister until, in April 1823, it voted 44–36, and on recount, 50–33, to pay Dexter $399 per year.[11] For the next two years, no difficulties over the minister arose.

Religious disputes arising during the same period in other towns led to even deeper, more permanent divisions. Trouble began in Kingston in 1801, when the town voted that a sum of $1,100 arising from the sale of pews in the meetinghouse be applied "for the support of a Congregational minister." Thereafter, the General Court incorporated seven men as trustees of the fund, but in 1803 a majority of the town voted to petition for a repeal of the incorporation act. As a result of the influence of a few prominent citizens, the act was not repealed, but much of the town seceded from the Congregational church and founded a new Baptist church. In 1805, the supporters of the act agreed to pay "every person that is dissatisfied with the ministerial fund their proportion of said fund," but that concession did not placate the newly organized Baptists. In 1805, they demanded and in 1812 finally received an exemption from the ministerial tax. In the words of the Congregationalist minister, the religious "discord and contention" of the first decade of the nineteenth century disrupted a "town . . . remarkable for [its] peace, unanimity and concord" and left the town permanently divided into competing religious factions.[12]

The story in Carver was somewhat similar. The town meeting first voted, 40–46, not to concur with the church in its choice of Lothrop Thompson as minister.[13] Apparently a compromise was reached and he was ordained, but five years later, in 1810, Baptists, who had founded a church in 1791, petitioned for an exemption from religious taxation. Twenty-seven residents protested against the exemption, which was not granted in 1810[14] but was granted in 1811, apparently before the passage of that year's Religious Freedom Act.[15] Five years later, in 1816, the town was again searching for a new minister.[16]

Most divisive of all were the events in neighboring Rochester. Trouble began when a committee report in 1788 showed that 36 families had not attended the town's church since the ordination of the Reverend Jonathan Moore and that only thirty out of the ninety-three families in the town were willing to contribute to his support.[17] Three years later, "[a]fter some debates," the town voted 29–18 to approve the result of an ecclesiastical council with Moore and then voted 47–1 not to continue his ministry.[18] A month later, by a vote of 40–18, the town approved the result of a council that had dissolved the relationship between Moore and the town.[19] Moore nevertheless continued to occupy the pulpit, even though the town refused to arbitrate its dispute with him, "there being a majority against" arbitration.[20] Finally, in May 1793, the town agreed to "Divide the Time Equally between the Reverd. Mr. Moors adherents & the other party & Each party agree to Supply the pulpit by Subscription if they think Best" and to have possession of the meetinghouse in alternate months.[21] This state of affairs continued for five years, until in 1798 one of the factions organized a new parish and church.[22] This division, however, cost the church its special place and power in a united Rochester community. Five years later, the old first parish decided to impose religious taxation "on those persons only that they supposed would willingly pay their Taxes,"[23] and nine years after that, in 1812, the parish "Voted to see if" the minister's "Salary could be obtained by Subscription."[24]

In short, during the years around 1800, a major transformation occurred in the structure of political and religious relationships in the towns of Plymouth County. Whereas most of them had been cohesive, insular communities in which neighbors had sought to minimize and accommodate their differences throughout most of the eighteenth century, they were now becoming mere geographic entities riven by conflicts that seemed incapable of being resolved. Moreover, as groups within the towns found themselves in long-term confrontations, they began to look for support from others in neighboring towns. In politics, this led to the formation of early political parties, whose members began to perceive some of their neighbors as adversaries and some outsiders as allies. A similar trend was apparent in religion, as Baptists, for example, established closer ties with their coreligionists in neighboring towns than with the Congregationalists in their own.

The causes underlying this transformation in the nature of people's relationships were, of course, complex,[25] but it is clear that the transformation was accentuated by the spread of commerce throughout Plymouth County, again during the years around 1800. Like religious dissenters and members of political organizations, men engaged in commerce relied on firm links to the outside world that often may have transcended their ties with their neighbors. Specific information about the trading connections of Plymouth's commercial residents is not readily available, but the evidence is ample for many other New England towns and there is no reason to think that patterns in Plymouth differed in any material way.

At the lower end of the social ladder, it appears that many of the individuals who have been categorized in this study as commercial were transients who resided in a single town only for a relatively brief period of time. One study of eighteenth-century Essex County has revealed that there was considerable migration in the eighteenth century into the growing commercial centers of Massachusetts, particularly the seaports, and that most migrants in the commercial towns worked as artisans, mariners, and laborers. Most of these migrants, moreover, preserved ties to other towns, did not become well integrated into the life of their new town, and, after a period of time, frequently moved on.[26] People of this sort, of course, would have been comparatively immune from communitarian forms of social control. Hence, their disputes would often have flowed to the courts.

Upper-class commercial men, notably merchants, also maintained strong ties with the outside world that may have weakened their connections with their own community. A major problem faced by eighteenth- and early nineteenth-century merchants was difficulty of communication.[27] A businessman in a mercantile center such as London or even Boston could not possibly keep abreast of changing market conditions in a town like Plymouth sufficiently to make his own marketing decisions. Men from distant ports who traded regularly with Plymouth needed associates there in whom they could repose total trust, just as Plymouth merchants trading in distant ports required associates in those places.

A common solution to the problem was the creation of a partnership, often among members of the same family, in which each partner managed the business of the firm in a different town. For example, Michael and Thomas Bull formed a partnership that maintained outlets in New York and Hartford, and Peter and Harris Colt created a similar arrangement to connect Hartford with Boston. Three Lyman brothers set up a slightly more complicated firm in the 1790s and early 1800s, with one partner managing the firm's interests in New York, another in Hartford, and the third in Vermont.[28] Partnerships could extend beyond mere trading ventures. For example, a merchant who wanted to insure his source of supply could enter into a partnership with a manufacturer, who would then continue to run the industrial establishment. Thus, the Dwights, a Springfield merchant family, became partners in both a distillery and a boating company in the 1790s.[29] Also common, particularly in the eighteenth century, were partnerships between merchants and fishermen, who supplied one of New England's most basic commodities for export. For example, when a merchant of little prominence named Edward Payne entered into a partnership with James Perkins of Boston to engage in the fish trade, Payne moved to Gloucester to be the fisherman, while Perkins, the supplier of the capital, remained in Boston to market the catch. Likewise, the Boston merchant Peter Faneuil sent a resident partner to abide in Canso, Nova Scotia, a major source of fish for New England's trade.[30]

Merchants also utilized other means to link themselves with commercial men in distant places. One was marriage. Silas Deane, for example, became a prominent mercantile figure by marrying into the Saltonstall family. Edmund Dwight enhanced his position by marrying into a leading Boston family, the Eliots. Another way in which a young man could establish contacts was by serving as an apprentice in a distant city. Thus, a Middletown merchant named Richard Alsop received his early training as an apprentice in New York, and another

Connecticut merchant, Thomas Mumford, sought to apprentice his son in Philadelphia.[31] The famous Peter Faneuil, who built the hall named after him in Boston, had been trained as a youth in New Rochelle, New York.[32]

When merchants lacked relatives or friends in a distant port, their final option was to establish a long-term agency relationship with another merchant there. For instance, Richard Derby, a leading Salem merchant of the pre-Revolutionary era, established a factorage relationship with Gardoqui & Co. of Bilboa, Spain, with whom he regularly traded, and a standing account with Lane & Fraser of London, who served as his bankers.[33] Likewise, Peter Faneuil maintained an extensive correspondence with Gulian Verplanck in New York and an account with Loyd & Lane of London. Most of the Faneuil business came to the family because the Faneuils were known to the whole commercial world as responsible factors.[34] There can be little doubt that they and others in agency relationships worked hard to sustain their reputations and that, in order to do so, they needed to give their full loyalty to the business interests of their principals.

Like members of political parties and religious dissenters, merchants thus introduced the divisions and competing values of the outside world into Plymouth County communities. Like the party members and religious dissenters, merchants had close allies in the outside world and often may have perceived their neighbors in adversarial roles. They also lived different lives than their agrarian neighbors. In short, merchants like political partisans and religious dissenters, destroyed a community's homogeneity. And, as Plymouth's towns lost their homogeneity, the institutions that had sprung from those towns—the town meeting, the local congregation, and the jury—lost their capacity to resolve conflicts and disputes in traditional ways. Each institution will now be considered in turn.

As in the pre-Revolutionary period, the location of schools and the boundaries of school districts were issues that often produced conflict in town meetings during the early nineteenth century. One such conflict arose in Plympton.[35] The first sign of a division within the town occurred at a June 1817 meeting, when it voted 13–21 not to act on a proposal relating to school districts.[36] Five months later, the town balloted 20–10 that school-district boundaries should remain as fixed by a committee report that had been accepted at a May 1817 meeting.[37] The division within the town grew closer, however, when at a December 1817 meeting, nine families were annexed to the town's fourth district by a 15–14 vote.[38] At a January 1818 meeting, the town voted not to reconsider the December vote, and, when this vote was disputed, the town again voted 25–31 not to reconsider.[39] The town then attempted to settle the quarrel between two rather evenly balanced factions by the eighteenth-century device of reference to an impartial committee, but, in November 1818, the committee's report was rejected, again on a close 12–13 vote.[40] As a result, the matter of Plympton's school-district boundaries was finally determined not by accommodation, as it likely would have been in the eighteenth century, but by the control a majority faction obtained over the town's political processes.

Another divisive issue arose when towns instructed their selectmen "to use their influence and exertions in their capacity to Suppress the evil of Intemperance."[41] The policies pursued by selectmen did not, however, always obtain unanimous assent. Thus, in Rochester, an attempt was made to have the town meeting overrule an 1819 selectmen's list of approved innholders, but the attempt was defeated by a 30–49 vote.[42] The voters of Rochester were also divided over the issue of fishing rights in the Mattapoisett River. In 1822, the town voted 36–17 to permit the taking of more fish than had been customary. This set off an extended controversy. First, the town balloted 23–29 not to limit the time of fishing to one day per week. Next, it voted 22–29 not to sell the fishing rights for the benefit of the entire town.[43] Two years later, it voted 31–49 not to consider anew the subject of fishing in the Mattapoisett River,[44] and soon thereafter decided 13–6 to fine an individual found guilty of violating the town's fishing regulations.[45] In other words, a group of Rochester residents interested in exploitation of the town's fish put together a series of majority votes by which they gained control of the local political process and turned it to their own economic ends.

Other significant economic issues were also determined by majority votes in town meetings in the period beginning in 1815. In Middleboro, for example, the petition of Seth Miller, Jr., for a public highway was defeated by a vote of 8–37,[46] and a private petition by one Calvin Pratt was defeated 14–172.[47] In Rochester, an effort by Ichabod Burges to terminate his guardianship was defeated by a vote of 11–33, after "a long and tedious debate."[48] One of the most curious matters was recorded in Plympton, which voted in November 1823 to leave in the hands of the selectmen the defense of a lawsuit about an "Irishman" brought against the town by Spencer Holmes.[49] A motion was made to reconsider this vote, and "[a] long debate ensued, and when the vote was put, it was after sunset, and so dark that the Town Clerk could not see to read or write." "[I]t was said that eleven persons voted for reconsidering, and seven against it," but "the moderator did not declare the vote; and for that reason the Town Clerk did not feel authorized to record it as a vote of the Town."[50]

In sum, during the three decades between the mid-1790s and the mid-1820s, the old eighteenth-century method of dispute settlement through accommodation and compromise broke down, and town meetings increasingly resolved conflicts by majority votes. Perhaps the change in practice can best be appreciated by comparing a 1796 entry in Bridgewater's records with one in 1821 from Duxbury. In 1796, before the old methods of accommodation and compromise had broken down, Bridgewater residents voted "to choose a Committee whose duty it shall be to report . . . such rules and regulations for the futer management of Town Meetings as they shall think will tend to give more general satisfaction and insure harmony" within the town.[51] Twenty-five years later, in Duxbury, however, efforts were no longer being made to give "general satisfaction and insure harmony," inasmuch as a warrant calling a town meeting simply directed the voters "to give in their votes by hand or polling the house."[52]

Efforts to obtain unanimous or nearly unanimous consent to the adjudication of disputes did not come to an end only in town meetings. Local church congregations also lost their ability to resolve disputes by eighteenth-century methods. Chapter 5 related how religious dissent spread to most towns in Plymouth County during the 1790s and early 1800s. The result of this phenomenon was that by 1810 it was no longer common, as it had been a half-century earlier, for nearly every inhabitant of a community to attend the local Congregational church. And, because of the increased number of religious dissenters, the church, which had been the principal institution engaged in extrajudicial dispute resolution, grew increasingly ineffective.

This is not to say that some churches did not attempt to impose discipline upon their members well into the nineteenth century. In Mattapoisett, for example, the church in 1804 suspended Caleb Dexter and in 1808 voted him "an heathen man and a publican" upon finding him guilty of "the sin of drunkenness."[53] In 1814, Nathaniel Hammond was excommunicated "for Intemperance,"[54] and Loice Handy, "having been guilty of fornication," was called upon "to repent of her sin before God and Make known to the Church her repentance." She was restored to "Peace with the Chh." only after she had done so.[55] Then, in 1818, Hannah Briggs was suspended "for unchastity" until the next year when she "exhibited satisfactory Evidence of Repentance."[56] In 1823, Isaac Tobey was excommunicated "for his Intemperance long persisted in,"[57] and Alice Meiggs was censured for failing to appear before the church to answer charges of "unchast & lascivious conduct" and theft.[58] Likewise, in Rochester in 1805, Aaron Hammond confessed to committing fornication.[59] In Middleboro, ecclesiastical proceedings were brought against at least six different individuals charged with intemperate drinking during the period from 1800 to 1825.[60]

Indeed, the Middleboro church continued to deal even with property and contract disputes, as in 1803 when Elkanah Elmes was excommunicated "on account of his unchristian conduct, in uttering falsehoods, & violating his promises"[61] and in 1826 when Thomas Pratt accused Leonard Elmes of improperly closing his dam and cutting off Pratt's water supply downstream.[62]

The largest number of post-Revolutionary disciplinary cases seems to have taken place in the town of Plymouth. The records suggest that there were at least four proceedings, the last occurring in 1814, against individuals failing to attend public worship,[63] and at least seven proceedings, the last in 1818, against church members charged with drunkenness.[64] In addition, there was a proceeding against two members charged with playing cards,[65] a proceeding against a woman charged with "*indecent*, *loose*, lascivious & *unchristian* Behavior,"[66] one against another man for "*rash & Profane Language*,"[67] a matter involving an alleged "*breach of Promise*,"[68] and a proceeding brought by a creditor against a widow "on Account of money which he thinks is justly due to him, from her late husband's Estate."[69]

Yet, despite these infrequent occasions upon which church discipline was successfully imposed, the fact remains that the enforcement of ecclesiastical discipline became an increasingly arduous task as the eighteenth century ended and the nineteenth began.[70] The growing difficulty of disciplining members is best evidenced, perhaps, by the fact that after the Revolution the largest number of disciplinary cases seems to have been brought, not against people charged with sexual immorality, excessive drinking, or breaches of Christian ethics in business dealings, but against individuals who left the Congregational order and joined a dissenting church.[71] For instance, in Rochester in the single year of 1782 Edward Morse was admonished for missing Communion, Mary Briggs for joining the Quakers, and George Hammond, for joining the Baptists;[72] and Isaac Snow, after confessing his guilt for "Speaking out & Calling ye Revd. Mr. Thomas West an *old Tory* while he was delivering a Sermon," petitioned to be dismissed to the Baptist church, which he probably joined even though his petition was denied.[73] Three years later, Hammond was again censured for joining the Baptists and Elnathan Crapo for missing church.[74] In 1791, Earl Clap was censured for having missed church for six years and having slandered the congregation's minister.[75]

Similarly, in Mattapoisett, Nathaniel Hammond was excommunicated in 1784 because he had "for a considerable Time neglected our Worship & Communion and gone after Sectaries."[76] In 1809, the church in Hanover sent a committee to converse with members who had neglected their religious duties. The committee reported, among other things, that "Josiah Chamberlain said he did not consider himself a member of the Church;" that "Joel Sylvester and wife said they did not consider themselves members of the church because they had joined themselves to a different denomination;" and that "Albert Smith's wife said in some respects she was a member of the Church and in some she was not, but on the whole she did not consider herself a member at present."[77] By 1810, the problem of defection to other sects had become so great that the Congregationalists were no longer able to proceed effectively against miscreants. All that the Congregationalist establishment could do "in case of a report that any member of this Church had joined himself or herself to any Church not in communion with this Church" was "inform the Person offending, that this Church will not, in future, consider or treat him or her as a Member of this Church."[78] As individuals left the established church during the 1810s and 1820s they were, in fact, no longer summoned to attend proceedings leading to their excommunication, but simply informed that their "Instability in the Christian Profession and breach of Covenant with this Church" rendered them "unfit to be considered any longer a Member of the body of Christ"[79] or that the local Congregational church "consider[ed] them as not belonging to our special communion, & not under the discipline of this Church"[80] and hence "exclude[d] . . . from visible membership with us."[81] Indeed, the Second Church of Scituate even granted a formal dismission to a woman who declared "that she could not in conscience commune with us, because the Pastor did not inculcate *total depravity—particular redemption—special grace—and Three Persons in one God*." As the church was told by a committee charged with investigating the affair, "this is all the apology that she offered, and probably all that could be obtained from her" and "an attempt to discipline in such case might occasion more evils tha[n] it would correct."[82]

The Congregational church lost its power to impose discipline not only upon those who actually left the church but also upon those who, while remaining in the church, were now free to leave if they felt injured or aggrieved. The Hanover church recognized as early as 1790 that the presence of nearby dissenting denominations limited its leverage over its own members when it voted that it was no longer "prudent to insist upon particular acknowledgments [of sin] in some certain cases when it is not done in others" because "many persons by this means are kept out of our Chhs & often join other persuasions."[83] Similarly when a group of Middleboro parishoners refused to attend church in 1816 because they were "dissatisfied with the Pastor of the Church," the congregation resolved "not to act, at present"[84]—a resolution to which the church adhered for at least two years.[85] Some years earlier, the Rochester church had faced up to the ineffectiveness of its discipline when James Cowing had commenced an ecclesiastical proceeding against its pastor, Jonathan Moore, because Moore had "sue[d] him . . . in Common Law for a Debt, wantonly & unnecessarily instead of trying to obtain redress . . . in a private manner or by laying ye matter before ye Church." The church, however, sanctioned Moore's action after concluding that he had been "under necessity to sue ye sd Cowing in order to obtain his just dues."[86] The problem that the church surely must have had in mind was illustrated in a proceeding several years later when Earl Clap was voted not to have acted "according to ye Simplicity & Integrity of a Christian" in that he "had in a Bargain . . . injured the

Truth."[87] But the injured individual obtained no redress because this Earl Clap was the same man who was censured three years later for not having attended church for six years.[88]

Thus, in many parishes ecclesiastical disciplinary proceedings simply came to a halt in the post-Revolutionary period.[89] In Hanover, for example, there appear to have been no disciplinary cases in the last quarter of the eighteenth century,[90] while both in Abington[91] and in Duxbury[92] the last case occurred in the early 1780s; in Wareham, the last two were in 1786[93] and 1791.[94] Finally, in North Bridgewater, the last cases occurred somewhat later, in 1806[95] and 1807.[96] Of course, as ecclesiastical procedures for the resolution of private disputes broke down, the only possibility for redress that many men had was to bring their disputes to court.

As litigants came to court, however, they found that its processes of dispute resolution were also undergoing change. In particular, juries in the first decade of the nineteenth century were losing the ability to reach unanimous verdicts as well as verdicts that were consistent with each other over time. In the opening years of the nineteenth century, litigants began to complain that juries exercised their power to find law in a manner that was "utterly indefinite and uncertain" and that provided litigants with "no rule for their future conduct."[97] It was argued that, when juries were given power to find law, "neither expedition, certainty nor system . . . prevailed."[98] Accordingly, it was urged "that juries ought by the court to be restrained and kept within proper and established rules."[99]

The Massachusetts courts responded between 1805 and 1810 by taking into their own hands the law-finding power that had previously belonged to juries. Around 1805, the Supreme Judicial Court began routinely to review alleged errors in the giving of instructions by judges and ultimately declared in 1808, that a judge was required to instruct the jury accurately. The courts also began the practice of setting aside verdicts that were contrary to their instructions. These changes made it clear by 1810 that judges determined the law and that juries decided only the facts.[100]

By the 1810s, then, the breakdown of eighteenth-century processes of dispute settlement through compromise, harmony, and unanimity was complete. Of course, the breakdown had begun much earlier—at least as early as the second quarter of the eighteenth century. As chapter 2 pointed out, few, if any, towns had ever acted with complete unanimity in all the matters that came before them in the first half of the eighteenth century. Certain matters, especially elections, were often decided by mere majority votes, and some towns even attempted, occasionally with success, to determine important substantive issues by less than unanimous votes. Chapter 3 also indicated that in several towns the church through much of the eighteenth century had enjoyed little success in resolving private conflicts and that, as a result, residents from those towns engaged frequently in litigation in the courts.

These early departures from what might be called a communitarian process of conflict resolution occurred, however, for much the same reason that the process broke down entirely in the early nineteenth century. The intrusion of outside forces and ideas into otherwise insular Plymouth communities led to the appearance of groups that were unwilling to have their disputes adjudicated by their adversaries in the towns in which they resided. Religious dissenters and schismatics, for example, were unwilling in both the eighteenth and nineteenth centuries to have the validity of their claims determined by local congregations whose value systems they no longer fully accepted. Similarly, the ties of commercial men to the outside world impaired their willingness to submit disputes to local churches.

In conclusion, then, the spread of commerce and religious dissent during the 1790s and early 1800s merely accelerated the work of forces that had already been at work for at least a century. The appearance of organized party politics produced much the same effect. In conjunction, the spread of commerce, religious dissent, and political conflict can be understood as bringing to an end the very possibility of genuine community in the sense of an all-inclusive group of neighbors who in isolation from the rest of the world lived by a single set of norms at both the ideal and the practical level—a form of community without which consensual dispute resolution by town meetings and local congregations could not be effectively conducted. The disruption of communitarian forms of life also undermined juries as institutions that were capable of resolving conflicts and disputes without direction and control from the bench on points of law. Thus, the intrusion into Plymouth County communities of outside, competing values and ways of life appears to have transformed the processes by which conflicts and disputes were resolved.

We can now appreciate what Kingston's minister may have meant when he remarked that his town had enjoyed "peace, unanimity and concord" throughout the eighteenth century. He could not have meant that the town was without conflict and dispute because every Plymouth County town almost certainly had its share. Instead, he probably meant that the residents of the old town had lived in isolation from divisive forces of the outside world, had shared a unitary value system and way of life, and had scarcely conceived that alternatives were possible. Not every town in eighteenth-century Plymouth County, of course, had had the same experience as Kingston. By 1825, few did.

Notes

Chapter 1

1. See William E. Nelson, *Americanization of the Common Law: The Impact of Legal Change on Massachusetts Society, 1760–1830* (Cambridge, Mass., 1975); Michael Zuckerman, *Peaceable Kingdoms: New England Towns in the Eighteenth Century* (New York, 1970).

2. See Kenneth A. Lockridge, *A New England Town: The First Hundred Years* (New York, 1970), 124, 135–36; David G. Allen, "The Zuckerman Thesis and the Process of Legal Rationalization in Provincial Massachusetts," *William and Mary Quarterly*, XXIX (3d ser. 1972), 443; John M. Murrin, "Review Essay," *History and Theory*, XI (1972), 226, 236–39, 250–54; L. Kinvin Wroth, "Possible Kingdoms: The New England Town from the Perspective of Legal History," *American Journal of Legal History*, XV (1971), 318.

3. See Robert W. Gordon, "Book Review," *New York University Law Review*, LI (1976), 686, 697; Murrin, "Review Essay," 266–68.

4. Anyone who reads the thousands of cases on which Nelson, *Americanization of the Common Law*, is based could not avoid being aware of the disputatiousness of eighteenth-century New Englanders.

5. Bridgewater, Duxbury, Hanover, Marshfield, Middleboro, Plymouth, and Scituate.

6. Plympton in 1707, Abington in 1712, Pembroke in 1712, Kingston in 1726, Halifax in 1734, and Wareham in 1739.

7. However, Hingham and Hull were taken out of Norfolk County and added to Plymouth in 1803.

8. Hanson, East Bridgewater, North Bridgewater (now Brockton), and West Bridgewater.

9. See Evarts B. Greene and Virginia D. Harrington, *American Population Before the Federal Census of 1790* (New York, 1932), xxiii, 21.

10. Only Boston, Marblehead, Salem, and Dartmouth were more populous.

11. See Jesse Chickering, *A Statistical View of the Population of Massachusetts, from 1765 to 1840* (Boston, 1846), 31–32.

12. See D. H. Hurd, *History of Plymouth County, Massachusetts* (Philadelphia, 1884), I, 319; II, 557, 674–75, 888.

13. See *ibid.*, II, 686–87, 862–64, 888, 1022–23.

14. See *ibid.*, II, 784, 1023, 1025; Thomas Weston, *History of the Town of Middleboro, Masachusetts* (Boston, 1906), 359–62, 426–27.

15. See Henry S. Griffith, *History of the Town of Carver, Massachusetts* (New Bedford, 1913), 1–2; Hurd, *History of Plymouth County*, I, 341.

16. See Hurd, *History of Plymouth County*, I, 330, 404.

17. See *ibid.*, II, 650.

18. *Ibid.*, II, 784.

19. See *ibid.*, II, 1024–25; Weston, *History of Middleboro*, 282–84, 287.

20. See Hurd, *History of Plymouth County*, I, 348.

21. See *ibid.*, I, 457; II, 1124A.

22. See Albert B. Hart, *Commonwealth History of Massachusetts* (New York, 1927–1930), III, 356, 526–45; IV, 408–19.

23. See Hurd, *History of Plymouth County*, I, 431; Samuel Deane, *History of Scituate, Massachusetts* (Boston, 1831), 47–55.

24. See Hurd, *History of Plymouth County*, I, 431. The town of Rochester never had a formal Quaker meeting in the eighteenth century. However, the present towns of Marion and Mattapoisett, then part of Rochester, each contain Quaker cemeteries; there is a meetinghouse at the Mattapoisett cemetery and the records of the

nearby Dartmouth meeting indicate that some meetings of that society were held in Rochester. See generally Birth, Death, and Marriage Records of the Dartmouth Monthly Meeting, 1699–1880, reel no. 51 (microfilm in possession of Rhode Island Historical Society, Providence, R.I.).

25. See Hurd, *History of Plymouth County*, II, 980–88. On the role of Backus, see generally William G. McLoughlin, *Isaac Backus and the American Pietistic Tradition* (Boston, 1967) and William G. McLoughlin, ed., *Isaac Backus on Church, State, and Calvinism: Pamphlets, 1754–1789* (Cambridge, Mass., 1968).

26. See generally Nelson, *Americanization of the Common Law.*

Chapter 2

1. See, e.g., Sprague v. Bowler, Ply. C.P., August 1760, no. 14.

2. See, e.g., Soule v. Soule, Ply. C.P., July 1769, no. 31.

3. Marshfield Town Records, 1700s, at 181 (ms. in Marshfield Town Hall, Marshfield, Mass.). Accord, Pembroke Town Records, 1735–91, II, 8 (ms. in Pembroke Town Hall, Pembroke, Mass.).

4. Rochester Town Records, I, 130 (ms. in Rochester Town Hall, Rochester, Mass.).

5. Annals of Kingston, quoted in D. H. Hurd, *History of Plymouth County, Massachusetts* (Philadelphia, 1884), I, 260. Accord, *Copy of the Old Records of the Town of Duxbury, Mass., from 1642 to 1770* (Plymouth, 1893), 274.

6. See Annals of Kingston, 260.

7. See *Old Records of Duxbury*, 274.

8. *Records of the Town of Plymouth* (Plymouth, 1892), II, 242.

9. *Ibid.*, II, 272. See also, e.g., Kingston Town Records, 1724–69, at 31 (ms. in Kingston Town Hall, Kingston, Mass.).

10. Annals of Kingston, 258. Accord, *Old Records of Duxbury*, 248; Plympton Town Records, I, 65 (ms. in Plympton Town Hall, Plympton, Mass.).

11. Halifax Town Records, 1734–98, at 49 (ms. in Halifax Town Hall, Halifax, Mass.).

12. *Records of Plymouth*, III, 48.

13. Bridgewater Town Records, 1739–84, III, 500 (ms. in Bridgewater Town Hall, Bridgewater, Mass.). For an example of a town's refusing to authorize a dam, see Pembroke Town Records, 1735–91, II, 29.

14. *Records of Plymouth*, II, 192.

15. Middleboro Town Records, 1746–72, at 197, 286 (ms. in Middleboro Town Hall, Middleboro, Mass.). See also *Records of Plymouth*, III, 251.

16. *Records of Plymouth*, III, 108.

17. *Ibid.*, III, 155.

18. *Ibid.*, III, 108. For an example of an adjudication of private rights in chattels arising out of a town's administration of the poor laws, see *Old Records of Duxbury*, 340.

19. Middleboro Town Records, 1746–72, at 205. Accord, *Records of Plymouth*, III, 42.

20. See, e.g., *Old Records of Duxbury*, 252; Marshfield Town Records, 1700s, at 69.

21. See, e.g., Bridgewater Town Records, 1739–84, III, 11; Scituate Records: Town Meeting Minutes, 1665–1742, at 98 (ms. in Scituate Town Hall, Scituate, Mass.); Wareham Town Records, 1739–1805, at 35 (ms. in Wareham Town Hall, Wareham, Mass.).

22. Marshfield Town Records, 1700s, at 181.

23. Pembroke Town Records, 1711–35, at 55.

24. Scituate Records: Town Meeting Minutes, 1665–1742, at 135.

25. Plympton Town Records, II, 26.

26. Middleboro Town Records, 1746–72, at 138.

27. Bridgewater Town Records, 1702–38, II, 112.

28. See, e.g., Middleboro Town Records, 1746–72, at 205.

29. See *ibid.*, 205.

30. *Records of Plymouth*, II, 21. See also *Old Records of Duxbury*, 199, where arbitrators who were discovered to have an interest in a matter were declared to be "incompetant judges." Cf. *Wrentham Proprietors* v. *Metcalf*, Quincy 36 (1763).

31. *Records of Plymouth*, III, 17–18. See also *ibid.*, II, 21, where the town clerk appears to have doubted the validity of a vote taken when "the people" had "almost withdrawn" from the meeting.

32. Records of the Second Church in Rochester, Parish Book, 50 (ms. in possession of First Congregational Church, Mattapoisett, Mass.).

33. Plympton Town Records, II, 3. See also *Records of Plymouth*, II, 282; Massachusetts Archives, CXIV, 251–52, quoted in Michael Zuckerman, *Peaceable Kingdoms: New England Towns in the Eighteenth Century* (New York, 1970), 159.

34. Middleboro Town Records, 1772–88, at 75.

35. *Records of Plymouth*, II, 238–39.

36. See *ibid.*, II, 240.

37. Massachusetts Archives, CXIV, 244–46, quoted in Zuckerman, *Peaceable Kingdoms*, 99.

38. *Records of Plymouth*, II, 242.

39. Plympton Town Records, I, 83.

40. *Ibid.*, I, 85.

41. *Ibid.*, II, 3.

42. *Ibid.*, II, 9.

43. *Ibid.*, II, 10.

44. Abington Town Records, I, Jan. 31, 1748/49 (ms. in Abington Town Hall, Abington, Mass.). See also *ibid.*, I, Feb. 9, 1747/48.

45. *Ibid.*, I, Aug. 31, 1749.

46. Halifax Town Records, 1734–98, at 118–19.

47. Hanover Town Records, 1727–99, at 169–70 (ms. in Hanover Town Hall, Hanover, Mass.).

48. Annals of Kingston, 260.

49. See, e.g., Halifax Town Records, 1734–98, at 88–90; Records of the First Parish, Scituate, 1761–1864, at 23 (ms. in Scituate Town Hall, Scituate, Mass.). But see, e.g., Halifax Town Records, 1734–98, at 8.

50. Annals of Kingston, 259. Accord, Halifax Town Records, 1734–98, at 123; Hanover Town Records, 1727–99, at 81; Records of the First Parish, Scituate, 1761–1864, at 4, 26; Wareham Town Records, 1739–1805, at 2.

51. *Old Records of Duxbury*, 314, 319.

52. Records of the Second Church in Rochester, Parish Book, 15.

53. Rochester Town [Precinct] Meetings, 1770–1869, at 12. For

evidence that towns and parishes labored at consensus building, see Records of the South Parish, Scituate, I, Oct. 11, 1750 (ms. in possession of First Unitarian Church, Norwell, Mass.), where the parish scheduled a day of fasting and prayer "to Look to God for His Blessing & Direction" in the choice of a new minister. Accord, *ibid.*, I, May 7, 1754.

54. Rochester Town [Precinct] Meetings, 1770–1869, at 12.

55. Bridgewater Town Records, 1739–84, III, 480.

56. Middleboro Town Records, 1772–88, at 65. See also Wareham Town Records, 1739–1805, at 12, where the town treasurer agreed to serve without compensation "for nothing but love and goodwill." For other examples of unanimous votes, see Bridgewater Town Records, 1739–84, at 130 (vote on care of town poor); Hanover Town Records, 1727–99, at 104 (vote on church pews), 116 (vote not to set off new town); *Records of Plymouth*, III, 63 (instructions to General Court representative re 1754 excise tax).

57. See e.g., Abington Town Records, Mar. 28, 1735 (vote on town boundary); Bridgewater Town Records, 1702–38, I & II, 246 (election of moderator); *ibid.*, 1739–84, III, 7 (vote not to set off new town); Halifax Town Records, 1734–98, at 8 (choice of minister); Hanover Town Records, 1727–99, at 64, 71, 92 (election of representative), 114 (vote not to send representative); Marshfield Town Records, 1700s, at 457 (location of future town meetings); *Records of Plymouth*, III, 93 (election of school committee), 140 (vote to require ministerial approval of schoolmasters); Plympton Town Records, I, 74 (election of town clerk); Records of the Second Church in Rochester, Parish Book, 13 (vote on minister's salary), 36 (vote on minister's salary).

58. *Old Records of Duxbury*, 274.

59. Bridgewater Town Records, 1702–38, I & II, 113.

60. Marshfield Town Records, 1700s, at 328. Accord, *ibid.*, 1779–1803, at 234, 253.

61. This and the following three paragraphs are based on William E. Nelson, *Americanization of the Common Law: The Impact of Legal Change on Massachusetts Society, 1760–1830* (Cambridge, Mass., 1975), 15–16.

62. See Petition of Dren, Ply. G.S., Oct. 1761.

63. Between 1781 and 1796, the major categories were fornication, 40 percent; paternity, 4 percent; crimes of violence, 14 percent; theft, 14 percent; liquor violations, 8 percent; refusing to serve in office, 3 percent; miscellaneous, 7 percent; and unknown, 9 percent. Between 1797 and 1825, the major categories were theft, 41 percent; crimes of violence, 23 percent; liquor violations, 10 percent; sex offenses, 7 percent; Sabbath breaches, 4 percent; miscellaneous, 12 percent; and unknown, 3 percent. These statistics, including those in the text, were gathered from General Sessions, Common Pleas, Superior Court, and Supreme Judicial Court records.

64. The statistics in the text are derived from a 10-percent sample of Common Pleas cases. See chapter 3, note 2, below. In the post-Revolutionary period, 1781–1825, 59 percent of all cases were for the collection of debts. This included actions of case on notes, which amounted to 49 percent of all litigation; actions of case on accounts which constituted 9 percent; actions of debt on bonds, which amounted to 1 percent; and actions to foreclose mortgages, which amounted to 0.1 percent. Land disputes accounted for 3 percent of all cases, as did suits for nondelivery of goods. Wage actions were 0.4 percent of the total, and defamation actions, 0.2 percent, and various miscellaneous actions added up to 5 percent. In 29 percent of all cases, the cause of action was insufficiently described for purposes of classification.

65. See Nelson, *Americanization of the Common Law*, 21.

66. See John M. Murrin, "Anglicizing an American Colony: The Transformation of Provincial Massachusetts" (Ph.D. dissertation, Yale Univ., 1966), 182–83.

67. Scituate Records: Town Meeting Minutes, 1743–80, at 19. Accord, e.g., Marshfield Town Records, 1700s, at 449; *Records of Plymouth*, III, 63.

68. The list of jurors was compiled from the names given in the court records at the beginning of each term of Common Pleas. No lists were compiled for the years prior to 1748 because the early court records did not indicate the town from which each juror came and, as a result, people from different towns having the same name

could not be distinguished. In the post-Revolutionary period, 1781–1825, 2,565 men served on juries.

69. In the post-Revolutionary period, 52 dissenters served on juries. Dissenters were identified from lists cited in chapter 3, notes 45, 74–75, below, and in chapter 5, notes 16, 35–36, below.

70. Out of a total population in 1765 of 23,119, approximately one-fourth, or 5,780, consisted of males over 21. See Evarts B. Greene and Virginia D. Harrington, *American Population Before the Federal Census of 1790* (New York, 1932), xxiii. The total number of men serving on juries between 1748 and 1774—1,613—is 28 percent of 5,780.

71. See Nelson, *Americanization of the Common Law*, 72–77.

72. See *ibid.*, 21–30.

73. See generally Emil Oberholzer, Jr., *Delinquent Saints: Disciplinary Action in the Early Congregational Churches of Massachusetts* (New York, 1956), 43–77, 127–63.

74. It appears that in the seventeenth century most offenses were normally punished by both civil and ecclesiastical authorities. See George L. Haskins, *Law and Authority in Early Massachusetts: A Study in Tradition and Design* (New York, 1960), 89. Although the incompleteness of church records makes certainty impossible, such does not appear to have been the case in the eighteenth century. It appears, instead, that civil and criminal matters were dealt with either by the state or by the church, and only rarely by both.

75. See Oberholzer, *Delinquent Saints*, 257.

76. See generally A Church Book . . . in the Fourth Church of Christ in Bridgewater, 1740–1832 (ms. in possession of First Parish Congregational Church, Brockton, Mass.).

77. *Ibid.*, 2.

78. See Halifax, Mass., Church Records, in *The Mayflower Descendant: A Quarterly Magazine of Pilgrim Genealogy and History* (Boston, 1899–1937), XXVI, 183; XXVII, 24, 30, 32; L. Vernon Briggs, *History and Records of the First Congregational Church, Hanover, Mass., 1727–1865* (Boston, Mass., 1895), I, 118, 120, 125, 131; Records of the First Church in Marshfield, Mass., in *Mayflower Descendant*, XXXI, 162; XXXII, 21; Marshfield Church Records, 1747–1850, at 160–61 (ms. in Marshfield Town Hall,

Marshfield, Mass.); Middleboro Church Records, 1708–1820, at 39 (ms. in possession of First Congregational Church, Middleboro, Mass.); Records of the Second Church in Rochester, Church Book, 29 (ms. in possession of First Congregational Church, Mattapoisett, Mass.).

79. See Halifax, Mass., Church Records, in *Mayflower Descendant*, XXVI, 184; XXVII, 33, 35, 185; Briggs, *Records of the Congregational Church, Hanover*, I, 127; Records of the First Church of Scituate, Mass., in *Mayflower Descendant*, XI, 208; Records of the First Church in Marshfield, Mass., in *Mayflower Descendant*, XI, 121, 122; XXXI, 119, 165; XXXII, 16; Marshfield Church Records, 1747–1850, at 160–61; Duxbury Church Records, 1729–1825, at 72 (ms. in possession of First Unitarian Church, Duxbury, Mass.); Records of the Church of Christ in the Joining Borders of Bridgewater and Middleboro, 13, 22 (microfilm in John Hay Library, Brown Univ.); Records of the Second Church in Rochester, Church Book, 23, 24.

80. See Halifax, Mass., Church Records, in *Mayflower Descendant*, XXVII, 35; Records of the First Church in Marshfield, Mass., in *Mayflower Descendant*, XI, 122; Abington Church Book, II, 9 (ms. in Dyer Memorial Library, Abington, Mass.); Middleboro Church Records, 1708–1820, at 39; Ancient Book of Records of the First Church of Christ of Rochester, I, 45–46 (ms. in possession of First Congregational Church, Rochester, Mass.); Records of the Second Church in Rochester, Church Book, 79.

81. Halifax, Mass., Church Records, in *Mayflower Descendant*, XXVII, 35.

82. Leonard H. Smith, Jr., *Records of the First Church of Wareham, Mass., 1739–1891*, at 19–21 (Clearwater, Fla., 1974).

83. Records of the Church of Christ in the Joining Borders of Bridgewater and Middleboro, 28.

84. Smith, *Records of the First Church of Wareham*, at 22–23.

85. Ancient Book of Records of the First Church of Christ in Rochester, I, 117.

86. *Ibid.*, I, 121–22.

87. *Ibid.*, I, 12.

88. Duxbury Church Records, 1729–1825, at 169–70.

89. *Ibid.*, 170.

90. See Halifax, Mass., Church Records, in *Mayflower Descendant*, XXVII, 29, 31, 34; Abington Church Book, II, 10; Duxbury Church Records, 1729–1825, at 170; Middleboro Church Records, 1708–1820, at 39; Ancient Book of Records of the First Church of Christ in Rochester, I, 20, 45–46; Records of the Second Church in Rochester, Church Book, 79; Smith, *Records of the First Church of Wareham*, at 19–21.

91. Middleboro Church Records, 1708–1820, at 19.

92. Smith, *Records of the First Church of Wareham*, at 26.

93. Halifax, Mass., Church Records, in *Mayflower Descendant*, XXVII, 32.

94. *Ibid.*, 34.

95. *Ibid.*, 33.

96. Middleboro Church Records, 1708–1820, at 36.

97. Records of the First Church in Marshfield, Mass., in *Mayflower Descendant*, XXXII, 12.

98. Halifax, Mass., Church Records, in *Mayflower Descendant*, XXVII, 27.

99. Abington Church Book, II, 15.

100. Briggs, *Records of the Congregational Church, Hanover*, I, 59.

101. Abington Church Book, I, Sept. 28, 1738.

102. Halifax, Mass., Church Records, in *Mayflower Descendant*, XXVII, 30.

103. Halifax, Mass., Church Records, in *Mayflower Descendant*, XXVII, 26, 32.

104. Duxbury Church Records, 1729–1825, at 71.

105. Abington Church Book, I, Jan. 3, 1722/23.

106. *Ibid.*, II, 11. See also note 74, above.

107. Smith, *Records of the First Church of Wareham*, at 23. See also note 74, above.

108. Ancient Book of Records of the First Church of Christ in Rochester, I, 95–96.

109. Smith, *Records of the First Church of Wareham*, at 23–24.

110. Ancient Book of Records of the First Church of Christ in Rochester, I, 148.

111. Smith, *Records of the First Church of Wareham*, at 28.

112. Abington Church Book, I, Sept. 17, 1741.

113. Ancient Book of Records of the First Church of Christ in Rochester, I, 131–32.

114. *Ibid.*, I, 15.

115. *Ibid.*, I, 137.

116. *Ibid.*, I, 124.

117. Smith, *Records of the First Church of Wareham*, at 25.

118. Middleboro Church Records, 1708–1820, at 8.

119. *Ibid.*, 39.

120. *Ibid.*, 39.

121. Duxbury Church Records, 1729–1825, at 75.

122. Ancient Book of Records of the First Church of Christ in Rochester, I, 50.

123. *Plymouth Church Records, 1620–1859* (New York, 1920), I, 293.

124. Ancient Book of Records of the First Church of Christ in Rochester, I, 102.

125. For example, when several brethren in Rochester voted against a church tax supported by the minister, he "suspended the administration of the Lord's Supper: But upon further weighing the case . . . [was] willing to Submit to the Judgment of the chh . . . [and] to administer the ordinance as usual" as soon as the church voted to do so. Ancient Book of Records of the First Church of Christ in Rochester, I, 45. The lack of clerical power was also displayed in Abington when the church was forced to leave a matter unresolved because the congregation was "equally divided 28 being on each side" with the "Pastor being unwilling to determine the question." Abington Church Records, III, Nov. 29, 1780.

126. Ancient Book of Records of the First Church of Christ in Rochester, I, 95.

127. Grand Jury Charge, Nantucket Super. Ct., Aug. 1746, in Cushing Papers, I (ms. in Massachusetts Historical Society, Boston, Mass.).

128. Grand Jury Charge, Nantucket Super. Ct., Aug. 1742, in *ibid.*

129. Smith v. Upham, Middlesex C.P., Sept. 1760 (rejecting quoted plea).

130. See *A Platform of Church Discipline Gathered out of the Word of God: and Agreed upon by the Elders: and Messengers of the Churches Assembled in the Synod at Cambridge in New England* (Cambridge, Mass., 1649), c. 10, sec. 5.

131. Ancient Book of Records of the First Church of Christ in Rochester, I, 92.

132. Records of the Second Church in Rochester, Church Book, 77.

133. *Plymouth Church Records*, I, 293–94.

134. Halifax, Mass., Church Records, in *Mayflower Descendant*, XXVII, 26.

135. Ancient Book of Records of the First Church of Christ in Rochester, I, 5–6.

136. *Ibid.*, I, 50.

137. Smith, *Records of the First Church of Wareham*, at 21.

138. See *ibid.*, 23.

139. See Halifax, Mass., Church Records, in *Mayflower Descendant*, XXVII, 26–27.

140. Abington Church Book, I, ca. Dec. 1722.

141. Records of the Second Church in Rochester, Church Book, 56.

142. Records of the Church of Christ in the Joining Borders of Bridgewater and Middleboro, 27, 29.

143. Duxbury Church Records, 1729–1825, at 178.

144. Smith, *Records of the First Church of Wareham*, at 28.

145. A Church Book . . . in the Fourth Church of Christ in Bridgewater, 1740–1832, at 84.

146. *Ibid.*, 70.

147. *Ibid.*, 70.

148. Records of the Church of Christ in the Joining Borders of Bridgewater and Middleboro, 19–20.

149. Records of the Second Church in Rochester, Church Book, 72.

150. *Ibid.*, 64.

151. Ancient Book of Records of the First Church of Christ in Rochester, I, 148.

152. Middleboro Church Records, 1708–1820, at 8.

153. Records of the Church of Christ in the Joining Borders of Bridgewater and Middleboro, 21.

154. Ancient Book of Records of the First Church of Christ in Rochester, I, 98.

155. *Ibid.*, I, 15.

156. Records of the Church of Christ in the Joining Borders of Bridgewater and Middleboro, 13.

157. Halifax, Mass., Church Records, in *Mayflower Descendant*, XXVII, 27.

158. Middleboro Church Records, 1708–1820, at 20–21.

159. Records of the Church of Christ in the Joining Borders of Bridgewater and Middleboro, 17.

160. *Ibid.*, 22.

161. Records of the Second Church in Rochester, Church Book, 64.

162. Halifax, Mass., Church Records, in *Mayflower Descendant*, XXVII, 27.

163. Records of the Second Church in Rochester, Church Book, 64.

164. Smith, *Records of the First Church of Wareham*, at 28.

165. See Oberholzer, *Delinquent Saints*, 36–42.

166. See *ibid.*, 35.

167. But see Ancient Book of Records of the First Church of Christ in Rochester, I, 176, for a proceeding brought by a resident of Wareham against a member of the Rochester church in that church. This is the only such proceeding in Plymouth County of which the author is aware.

168. For a full discussion of the history of Puritan ideas about church membership, see Edmund S. Morgan, *Visible Saints: The History of a Puritan Idea* (Ithaca, N.Y., 1963).

169. Halifax, Mass., Church Records, in *Mayflower Descendant*, XXVII, 28–29. It is not clear whether every adult resident of a parish had received baptism, and patterns may have varied from

parish to parish. See generally Oberholzer, *Delinquent Saints*, 24–25.

170. See Thomas Lechford, *Plain Dealing: or, Newes From New England*, in *Collections of the Massachusetts Historical Society* (3rd ser.), III (1833), 55, 73–74.

Chapter 3

1. This figure is correct within a range of 67 to 72 percent with a 95-percent level of confidence. The percentages are derived from the numbers reported in notes 2–5, below, and accompanying text.

2. The intracommunity total, 2,537, was calculated by counting all Common Pleas cases during the period 1725–74 in which all parties were residents of the same Plymouth County town, and, in the case of Bridgewater, Middleboro, Plympton, Rochester, and Scituate, by multiplying the total for each town by an intracommunity proportion derived from a sample of cases for each town. The total is correct within a range of 2,360 to 2,743 with a 95-percent level of confidence. See notes 12, 21, 25, 68 and 70, below, and accompanying text. The total number of intracounty cases, 8,360, was derived by multiplying by 10 the number of cases involving only residents of Plymouth County contained in a random 10-percent sample of all Common Pleas cases. The sample was obtained by recording and coding for every tenth case information on the residence and social class or occupation of each litigant and on the nature of the cause of action.

3. This figure constitutes the sum of all intratown cases for Hanover, Pembroke, and Plymouth and intracommunity cases for Rochester and Scituate. It is correct within a range of 1,686 to 1,893 cases with a 95-percent level of confidence. See notes 68 and 70, below, and accompanying text.

4. This and all other statements about population are based on data contained in table 1.1. In this chapter, all references are to population figures reported in the census of 1765. For a discussion of the utility of those figures for purposes of the comparative analysis presented in this chapter, see note 29, below.

5. This figure is derived from table 3.1 and the accompanying

footnotes. It is correct within a range of 645 to 850 cases with a 95-percent level of confidence.

6. See William G. McLoughlin, *New England Dissent, 1630–1833: The Baptists and the Separation of Church and State* (Cambridge, Mass., 1971), I, 124 n. 23; Emil Oberholzer, Jr., *Delinquent Saints: Disciplinary Action in the Early Congregational Churches of Massachusetts* (New York, 1956), 43–44.

7. The Titicut parish, however, is treated in effect as two communities, one being that portion of the parish that lay in Bridgewater and the other being the portion that lay in Middleboro. Once it has been determined that a litigant resided in Titicut, it is easy to determine the portion of the parish in which he lived because court records always state a litigant's residence by town.

8. Namely, the Center and West parishes. Records for the East Parish also appear to be incomplete. See Harold F. Worthley, *An Inventory of the Records of the Particular (Congregational) Churches of Massachusetts Gathered 1620–1805* (Cambridge, Mass., 1970), 121–22, 196–97, 661–62.

9. Williams Latham, *Epitaphs in Old Bridgewater, Massachusetts* (Bridgewater, 1882).

10. Titicut Parish and Alden cemeteries.

11. The seven cemeteries are located at the corner of Main St. and Ashland St.; on the west side of Main St. near the intersection of Grove St.; on the west side of Summer St. about 1,000 feet north of Plain St.; on the south side of Pine St. near the intersection of Quincy St.; on the south side of Pleasant St. about 1,000 feet west of West St.; on the south side of Mill St. near the intersection of Belmont St.; and on the west side of Pearl St. about 1,000 feet north of Pleasant St. Another cemetery with eighteenth- and early nineteenth-century graves, which is near the intersection of Belmont St. and West St., was not examined because access could not be obtained. Other cemeteries in the town are modern.

12. This estimated proportion, or percentage, of intracommunity cases, .36, is correct within a range of .25 to .47 with a 95-percent level of confidence. For the formula used to calculate the precision of this estimate of the intracommunity proportion of Bridgewater

cases, see William Cochran, *Sampling Techniques* (New York, 1963), 73–75. The formula is

$$d = t\sqrt{\frac{N - n}{N - 1}\quad\frac{pq}{n}}$$

where p = the relevant proportion in the sample, in this case the percentage of all cases that were of an intracommunity nature; q = 1 − p; n = the number of cases in the sample; N = the number of cases in the total population from which the sample was taken; d = the margin of error of the proportion, or the number which when added to or subtracted from the sample proportion gives the range of values of that proportion; and t = a value in the normal distribution table that corresponds to a certain chosen level of confidence for the sample proportion. For the table used in the derivation of t in this calculation and all others in this study, see Paul G. Hoel, *Elementary Statistics* (New York, 1966), 329, table IV. The level of confidence chosen here was 95 percent; that is, in only 5 percent of all random samples of this size would the variation in the proportion be greater than the range of values here calculated.

13. See generally Douglas L. Jones, "Geographic Mobility and Society in Eighteenth-Century Essex County, Massachusetts" (Ph.D. dissertation, Brandeis Univ., 1975), 87–102, 119–21, 140–41.

14. See table 3.1, which shows that Bridgewater had one of the county's lower intracommunity litigation rates and that, even if the rate were doubled, the rates of three of the nine nonlitigious towns in the table would still be higher.

15. See D. H. Hurd, *History of Plymouth County, Massachusetts* (Philadelphia, 1884), II, 1022. For the history of the two main river settlements, Muttock and Four Corners Village, see Thomas Weston, *History of the Town of Middleboro, Massachusetts* (Boston, 1906), 272–302, 355–85.

16. See Weston, *History of Middleboro*, 447–49.

17. From 1725 to 1740, Middleboro had 8 percent of the county's intratown litigation. In 1741, it had 15 percent; in 1742, 17; in 1743, 23; in 1744, 25; in 1745, 18; in 1746, 30; in 1747, 18; and in 1748, 20. Between 1749 and 1774, Middleboro had 14 percent of the county's total.

18. See Weston, *History of Middleboro*, 284, 328.

19. See Gravestone Records from the Old Cemetery at "the Green," Middleborough, Mass., in *The Mayflower Descendant: A Quarterly Magazine of Pilgrim Genealogy and History* (Boston, 1899–1937), XII, 65–71, 142–45, 198–202; XIII, 23–27, 117–20; XIV, 80–85, 130–36, 214–24; Records from the Nemasket Cemetery, Middleborough, Mass., in *ibid.*, XV, 1–9, 100–110. Those buried in the cemetery at the Green are treated as residents of the Center Parish community, and those at rest in Nemasket Cemetery are treated as residents of the river settlements.

20. People buried in the Titicut Parish and Alden cemeteries, both on Plymouth St. in North Middleboro, were treated as residents of Titicut Parish. Anyone buried in the eight following Lakeville cemeteries was considered to be a resident of the Lake Parish: Pond, Thompson Hill, Canedy, Haskins, Keith, Sampson, and the cemeteries at the Mullein Hill Baptist Church and on Route 105 south of the intersection of Route 18. All who were buried in the following four cemeteries were treated as residents of the Center Parish community: on Summer St. between Murdock St. and Plymouth St., on Vaughan St. west of Cherry St., at the intersection of Marion Rd. and Perry St., and the one at the Methodist Church in South Middleboro.

21. Using the same formula as used in note 12, above, with a 95-percent confidence level and p = .37, the range of the percentage of intracommunity cases in Middleboro is between 27 and 47 percent.

22. See Hurd, *History of Plymouth County*, II, 1109.

23. See Gravestone Records in the Old Cemetery at Plympton, Mass., in *Mayflower Descendant*, VIII, 150–54; IX, 117–19, 214–17; X, 111–16, 144–49, 217–21; XI, 115–19, 161–65, 194–98; Gravestone Records in a Small Cemetery in the North Village of Plympton, Mass., in *ibid.*, XI, 176–77.

24. Three of the cemeteries are located along Route 58: Union and the ones at the intersection of Linton Drive and adjacent to the First Baptist Church. The fourth cemetery is located along Route 44 near the Plymouth town line.

25. Using the same formula as used in note 12, above, with a 95-percent confidence level and p = .88, the range of the percentage of intracommunity cases in Plympton is between 75 and 99.5 percent.

26. See Hurd, *History of Plymouth County*, II, 1164.

27. Published records are available for four cemeteries in Marshfield's South Parish. See Records from the Old Burial Ground at the Congregational Church, Marshfield, in *Mayflower Descendant*, XII, 54–56, 148–50, 251; XIII, 46–50, 109–11, 129–34; Gravestone Records in the Cemetery at Marshfield Centre, Mass., in *ibid.*, VIII, 196; Records from the Cemetery near the Congregational Chapel, Marshfield, Mass., in *ibid.*, XIII, 241–47; Records from the "Plainville Cemetery," Marshfield, Mass., in *ibid.*, XIV, 48–52. Records are published for three cemeteries in the North, or Marshfield Hills, Parish. See Gravestone Records from the Cemetery at Marshfield Hills, Mass., in *ibid.*, IX, 92–96, 167–71, 203–6; Gravestone Records from the "Two Mile" Cemetery, Union Street, North Marshfield, Mass., in *ibid.*, X, 246–49; Records from the "Little" Cemetery at Sea View, Marshfield, Mass., in *ibid.*, XI, 70–73. The 15-case sample, in which there were eight intraparish and seven interparish cases, was gathered from these published records. Using the same formula as used in note 12, above, with a 95-percent confidence level and $p = .53$, the range of the percentage of intraparish cases in Marshfield is between 31 and 75 percent—a range that is too large to permit useful estimates.

28. Given the central conclusion of this chapter that the litigation rate of Marshfield was low in comparison with those of certain other towns, it is preferable to err in the direction of overestimating rather than underestimating its litigation.

29. Population data are for the year 1765, as reported in table 1.1. No other population figures are available during the period 1725–74. Therefore, the number of cases reported per year per 1,000 persons becomes increasingly inaccurate toward the earlier years of the pre-Revolutionary period, when it is almost certain that each town's population was much smaller than in 1765. The figures seem reasonably accurate, however, for comparative purposes, which are the only purposes for which they are used in the subsequent analysis. Although population figures are not available prior to 1765, figures indicating each town's percentage of the county tax are available for forty years during the fifty-year period. These percentages, which

were set by the General Court annually on the basis of each town's population and landed wealth—see, e.g., Laws of 1733–34, c. 3, sec. 3 (1733), in *The Acts and Resolves, Public and Private, of the Province of the Massachusetts Bay* (5 vols., Boston, 1878), II, 684; Laws of 1743–44, c. 9, sec. 3 (1743), in *ibid.*, III, 98; Laws of 1757–58, c. 2, sec. 3 (1757), in *ibid.*, IV, 15—remained relatively constant from 1728 on.

The following table gives each town's percentage of the 1765 population and its highest and lowest percentages of the county tax rate between 1728 and 1774:

	Percent of 1765 Population	*Percent of County Tax: Low–High*
Bridgewater	17%	14–19%
Middleboro	15%	9–15%
Scituate	11%	12–17%
Plymouth	9%	8–13%
Rochester	8%	6–10%
Pembroke	6%	4– 7%
Plympton	6%	5– 8%
Abington	5%	2– 7%
Marshfield	5%	5–10%
Hanover	5%	3– 5%
Duxbury	5%	4– 6%
Kingston	3%	3– 4%
Halifax	2%	2– 3%
Wareham	2%	1– 3%

As the table shows, in all but four towns, each town's percentage of the county tax never varied more than 3 points from its percentage of the 1765 population. In the four towns where greater variation occurred, much of it can be explained by the fact that tax rates reflected wealth as well as population. For example, Marshfield, Plymouth, and Scituate paid a larger portion of the 1765 tax than their percentage of the population warranted: Marshfield, with 5 percent of the population, paid 7 percent of the tax; Plymouth, with 9 percent of the population, paid 10 percent of the tax; and Scituate, with 11 percent of the population, paid 14 percent of the tax. It is likely that these three wealthy towns always paid a larger portion of the tax than their population alone warranted, for if their 1765 tax rates are taken as the base, there is never more than a 3-point variation from that rate during the entire 1728–74 period. Likewise, Middleboro, with 15 percent of the population, paid only 13 percent of the taxes in 1765. The unusually low rates of this town throughout the period probably reflect its relative poverty because the variation between its 13-percent rate in 1765 and its lowest rate, 9 percent, is only 4 points.

30. Except 1734–74 for Halifax, 1726–74 for Kingston, and 1739–74 for Wareham.

31. The numbers in the table for Bridgewater are estimates based on note 12, above. They are correct with a 95-percent confidence level within a range of 101 to 190 for total cases, of 2.02 to 3.80 for cases per year, and of 0.51 to 0.96 for cases per year per 1,000 inhabitants.

32. The numbers in the table for Middleboro are estimates based on note 21, above. They are correct with a 95-percent confidence level within a range of 119 to 206 for total cases, of 2.38 to 4.12 for cases per year, and of 0.70 to 1.21 for cases per year per 1,000 inhabitants.

33. The numbers in the table for Plympton are estimates based on note 25, above. They are correct with a 95-percent confidence level within a range of 89 to 118 for total cases, of 1.78 to 2.36 for cases per year, and of 1.28 to 1.70 for cases per year per 1,000 inhabitants.

34. Population figures are for the year 1765. See note 29, above, for an explanation of why those figures are used.

35. Those appearing in litigation on only one or two occasions in their lives were placed in a separate category because there seemed to be a natural break in most towns between the numbers of those

appearing only once or twice and those appearing more frequently. As table 3.2 shows, a sizable portion of the population of most towns appeared in court on 1 or 2 occasions, but rather few appeared more frequently. Those appearing on 8 or more occasions were placed in a separate category because it was decided to obtain biographical information on the most litigious people. Drawing the line at 8 gave a total of 193 individuals, or 7 percent of all litigants, for whom information was needed. Drawing the line at 7 would have made it necessary to obtain information on another 2 percent of all litigants.

36. Middleboro Church Records, quoted in Weston, *History of Middleboro*, 444.

37. See *ibid.*, 445.

38. See *Copy of the Old Records of the Town of Duxbury, Mass. from 1642 to 1770* (Plymouth, 1893), 240, 246, 248, 249, 251, 291, 293, 301, 317.

39. Weston, *History of Middleboro*, 274.

40. See Hurd, *History of Plymouth County*, II, 953.

41. All 49 of these highly litigious individuals came from five of the nine towns: Bridgewater, Duxbury, Kingston, Middleboro, and Plympton. Information on officeholding was obtained for Bridgewater, Kingston, and Middleboro from lists published in Hurd, *History of Plymouth County*, I, 286–88; II, 545–46, 811–12, 839, 920–21, 952–58. In addition, the name of every highly litigious individual in Bridgewater was checked in Nahum Mitchell, *History of the Early Settlement of Bridgewater* (Boston, 1840), through use of the index. The same was done for highly litigious individuals in Middleboro in Weston, *History of Middleboro*. Information on Duxbury was obtained by checking the name of every highly litigious individual through the index of *Old Records of Duxbury*. Information on the one highly litigious resident of Plympton was obtained from the Plympton Town Records (ms. in Plympton Town Hall, Plympton, Mass.).

42. See Weston, *History of Middleboro*, 228–29.

43. See Edward M. Cook, *The Fathers of the Towns: Leadership and Community Structure in Eighteenth-Century New England*

(Baltimore, 1976), 24–35. He estimates that in towns of about 1,200 people or less, approximately three-fourths of the adult males held some office during their lives.

44. This statement is based on the plaque on the front of the meetinghouse, which is still standing.

45. Litigants have been identified as Quakers on the basis of marriage records in a book of Quaker records in the custody of the Pembroke town clerk. These records list the names of all members of the meeting attending every marriage ceremony.

46. Pembroke Monthly Meeting, Men's Meeting, 1702–1830, Jan. 1, 1737 (microfilm reel no. 49, Rhode Island Historical Society, Providence, R.I.).

47. *Ibid.*, Dec. 4, 1735.

48. *Ibid.*, Jan. 3, 1735.

49. Approximately 300 individuals who resided in Pembroke and Hanover and occasionally in neighboring towns have been identified as members of the Pembroke meeting during the entire period 1725–74. The combined population of Pembroke and Hanover was 2,493 in 1765.

50. These averages for the new period 1725–39 have not been adjusted for population because reliable population data are not available prior to the 1765 census.

51. In Pembroke, there were 35 cases involving only Quakers and 67 involving litigation between Quakers and Congregationalists in the period 1725–39. There were 8 cases involving only Quakers and 41 cases between Quakers and Congregationalists in the years 1740–74. In Hanover, there was 1 case involving only Quakers and 31 involving both Quakers and Congregationalists between 1725 and 1739. There were 2 cases involving only Quakers and 19 involving members of both denominations between 1740 and 1774.

52. See McLoughlin, *New England Dissent*, I, 225–36.

53. A question that arises is why Quakers and other dissenters were willing to accept resolution of disputes by juries in courts, particularly in the eighteenth century, when the juries that decided cases were likely to be composed of people who were little different from those sitting on local congregations and who probably decided cases

by reference to the same norms regardless of the institution they served. There are two possible reasons. One is that, once the cheaper and more convenient institution, the church, had been undermined, an individual seeking to resolve a dispute had no place to go other than a court. The other reason is that a jury randomly drawn from all fourteen of the county's towns would be further removed from whatever gave rise to a dispute than a local congregation and perhaps be somewhat less partisan. It is noteworthy that the eighteenth-century law of evidence, which reflected prevailing assumptions about human nature, prohibited persons with an "Interest . . . ever so small" from testifying in an action. *Wrentham Proprietors* v. *Metcalf*, Quincy 36 (1763). The concept of a preclusive interest, moreover, was so broad that a member of a municipal corporation subject to taxation was barred, for example, from testifying in a lawsuit involving the corporation, see *ibid.*, and all Baptists were precluded in another case from giving testimony in reference to an allegedly unlawful collection of a tax from a coreligionist on the theory that they might gain or lose from any precedent that a jury verdict would set. See L. Kinvin Wroth and Hiller B. Zobel, eds., *Legal Papers of John Adams* (Cambridge, Mass., 1965), II, 36–37 n. 8. Surely a person who could not be trusted to "act with . . . deliberation and judgment," *ibid.*, III, 232 (argument of counsel), in giving testimony would not be favored as an adjudicator. Because it seems likely that church members might have had at least slim ties of interest with a fellow member involved in a dispute with a dissenter or schismatic, it is understandable that such a litigant would prefer adjudication of his disputes by jurors who, because they were drawn from distant towns, might have had either weaker ties to his adversary or none at all.

54. See Hurd, *History of Plymouth County*, I, 241.

55. See John S. Barry, *A Historical Sketch of the Town of Hanover, Mass., with Family Genealogies* (Boston, 1853), 338, 386.

56. See Hurd, *History of Plymouth County*, I, 178.

57. Because the Manomet church consisted of only 25 members in 1747, see *ibid.*, I, 178, it seems unlikely that the total population of the community exceeded 200.

58. Indeed, a search of the gravestones in the cemetery at the Manomet church identified only one individual buried there who attained his majority prior to 1774.

59. It is impossible on the basis of information contained in the writs to categorize more than 28 percent of Plymouth's pre-Revolutionary intratown cases as involving a substantively commercial issue. This categorization presupposes that 11 actions of case for nondelivery of goods and 236 actions of case upon accounts were all of a commercial nature. There is no evidence in the court records that any other cases involved commercial issues, though some of them surely did. A more promising approach is to categorize cases as commercial on the basis of occupations of the parties. Thus 258 of Plymouth's 891 cases involved at least one party identified as a merchant, dealer, trader, or shopkeeper. When seamen are added, another 217 cases are accounted for, and the addition of another 208 cases involving at least one party engaged in manufacturing brings the total to 683. This broad definition is the only one that places enough cases in the commercial category to account for the difference in litigation rates between Plymouth and the county's other towns.

60. In Hanover and Pembroke, all intratown cases have been treated as intracommunity for purposes of this study.

61. The numbers for Plympton are estimates derived by multiplying the total number of noncommercial cases by the percentage of intratown cases that were intracommunity in nature. See notes 25 and 33, above. They are correct with a 95-percent confidence level within a range of 73 to 97 cases for total noncommercial cases and within a range of 1.05 to 1.40 for cases per year per 1,000 residents.

62. The numbers for Middleboro are estimates derived by multiplying the total number of noncommercial cases by the percentage of intratown cases that were intracommunity in nature. See notes 21 and 32, above. They are correct with a 95-percent confidence level within a range of 82 to 142 cases for total noncommercial cases and within a range of 0.48 to 0.83 for cases per year per 1,000 residents.

63. The numbers for Bridgewater are estimates derived by multiplying the total number of noncommercial cases by the percentage of

intratown cases that were intracommunity in nature. See notes 12 and 31, above. They are correct with a 95-percent confidence level within a range of 83 to 157 cases for total noncommercial cases and within a range of 0.42 to 0.80 for cases per year per 1,000 residents.

64. See text at notes 56–58, above. The fact that Plymouth was the county seat and that litigation did not require travel to another town might also have given it a slightly higher litigation rate than most of the county's other towns.

65. Information on offices was obtained from lists published in D. H. Hurd, *History of Plymouth County*, I, 115–20, and by checking names of litigious individuals in volumes 2 and 3 of *Records of the Town of Plymouth* (Plymouth, 1892–1903) through use of the indices.

66. See *ibid.*, III, 164, 172.

67. Not only did commercial and upper-class litigants appear more frequently in intracommunity litigation in Plymouth than in the county's nonlitigious towns; there is also some evidence that they made a higher percentage of their appearances as plaintiffs. To obtain quantitative data about the social class of litigants, intratown cases from both Plymouth and the nine nonlitigious towns were selected in which at least one party on each side fit within one of the following seven categories: esquire, gentleman, merchant, farmer, seaman, transportation worker, or laborer. For further definition of these categories, see chapter 4, note 6, below. Using the cases so selected, two measures were created. One measure identified as upper-class litigants those who bore the title of esquire, gentleman, or merchant; and as lower class those who were named as farmer, seaman, transportation worker, or laborer. This measure generated a sample of 180 cases between the two classes in the nine nonlitigious towns, in which upper-class plaintiffs appeared against lower-class defendants 73 percent of the time, and a sample of 226 interclass cases in Plymouth, in which upper-class litigants were plaintiffs 83 percent of the time. A second measure identified as lower class only the three lowest of the above named groups—seamen, transportation workers, and laborers—and identified the remaining four groups as being upper class. This second measure generated a sample of 148

interclass cases in the nine nonlitigious towns, in which upper-class litigants were plaintiffs 70 percent of the time, and a sample of 194 interclass cases in Plymouth, in which the upper class appeared as plaintiffs in 82 percent of the cases. By either measure, upper-class litigants were more likely to appear as plaintiffs in Plymouth than in the nonlitigious towns. Moreover, because plaintiffs won 90 percent (±2 percent) of all cases in the county during the pre-Revolutionary period, including 66 percent (±6 percent) of all contested cases—estimates which are made with a 95-percent level of confidence pursuant to the formula given in note 12, above—it is also likely that upper-class litigants won a higher percentage of the cases in Plymouth than they did in the county's nonlitigious towns.

68. The sample was derived from published lists of those buried in three cemeteries (see Gravestone Records from the Private Burial Ground of the James Family, at Greenbush, Scituate, Mass., in *Mayflower Descendant*, X, 27–28; Gravestone Records from the Old Burying Ground at Meeting House Lane, Scituate, Mass., in *ibid.*, VIII, 115–18; Gravestone Records from the Old Second Church Cemetery, Norwell, Massachusetts, in *ibid.*, XXXII, 107–11) and from lists drawn up from gravestones in three cemeteries in Scituate: Fairview, the cemetery on Mann Lot Rd. near the intersection of Country Way, and the one on Clapp Road; and from four in Norwell: First Parish, Pinehurst, Stockbridge, and the cemetery on Route 123 at the Norwell-Hanover line. Individuals buried in modern Scituate were treated as residents of the First Parish, and those in Norwell as residents of the Second. Using the same formula as used in note 12, above, with a 95-percent level of confidence and p = .47, the range of the percentage of intracommunity cases in Scituate is between 34 and 60 percent.

69. Unfortunately, there is no good town history for Rochester describing relationships between the different parts of the town. The reason for dividing the First Parish in this manner is that Marion encompassed a maritime community that lay along the sea, whereas Rochester Center was an inland, agrarian community.

70. Because no cemetery records have been published for any portion of the original town of Rochester, the 79-case sample was

generated entirely from lists drawn up from gravestones. In Mattapoisett, seven cemeteries were examined: Barlow, Cushing, Ellis, Hammond, Mendell, Pine Island, and Quaker. In Marion, six cemeteries were studied: Evergreen, Friends', Little Neck, North, Old Landing, and the one on Point Rd. between Cross Neck Rd. and Delano Rd. In Rochester Center, four cemeteries were examined: Center, Hillside, Sherman, and Woodside. In North Rochester, three were studied: Ashley, North, and Old Parish. In Wareham, three cemeteries were also examined: Long Neck, and the ones at the intersection of Stillman Memorial Dr. and Great Neck Rd. and on Tihonet Rd. near the intersection of Route 28. Using the same formula as used in note 12, above, with a 95-percent confidence level and p = .47, the range of the percentage of intracommunity cases in Rochester is between 37 and 57 percent.

71. The estimates for Scituate and Rochester were derived by multiplying the number of noncommercial cases in each town by the percentage of intratown cases that were intracommunity in nature.

72. The list of Scituate Quakers, who attended the Pembroke meeting, is compiled from the marriage records in a book of Quaker records in the custody of the Pembroke town clerk. The records list the names of all adult members of the meeting attending every marriage ceremony.

73. The numbers for Rochester are estimates based on note 70, above. They are correct with a 95-percent confidence level within a range of 100 to 154 cases for total noncommercial cases and within a range of 1.03 to 1.59 cases per year per 1,000 residents.

74. The numbers for Scituate are estimates based on note 68, above. They are correct with a 95-percent confidence level within a range of 96 to 168 cases for total noncommercial cases and within a range of 0.77 to 1.35 cases per year per 1,000 residents.

75. The list of Rochester Quakers is compiled from the microfilm collection of Quaker records held by the Rhode Island Historical Society, Providence, R.I. The following records were used: the Birth, Death, and Marriage Records of the Dartmouth Monthly Meeting, 1699–1880 (microfilm reel no. 51); the Birth, Death, and Marriage Records of the Sandwich Monthly Meeting, 1646–1761 (microfilm

reel no. 44); and the Marriage Records of the Sandwich Monthly Meeting, 1762–1841 (microfilm reel no. 44). The records of marriages include the names of all adult members of the meeting who attended the ceremonies.

76. See Charles S. Hamlin et al., *Mattapoisett and Old Rochester, Massachusetts* (New York, 1907), 192–95.

77. Records of the Second Church in Rochester, Church Book, 56 (ms. in possession of First Congregational Church, Mattapoisett, Mass.).

78. The sample indicates that 11 out of 19 cases, or 58 percent, occurred during the five-year period. The accuracy of this sample was checked by using the following formula from William Cochran, *Sampling Techniques* (New York, 1963), 73–75:

$$d = t\sqrt{\frac{pq}{n}}$$

This formula is a variant of that used in note 12, above. With a 95-percent level of confidence and p = .58, the range in the percentage of all Mattapoisett intracommunity litigation that occurred during the schism is between 36 and 80 percent.

79. The list of officeholders in Scituate was compiled from a set of files in the Scituate town hall that lists the name of every officeholder in the town together with the offices he held.

80. According to the Rochester town clerk, town meeting records that would list all officeholders do not exist for a period from the early 1730s to the early 1770s. The author was not permitted to enter the vault where the records are stored, and hence the town clerk's statement has not been verified.

Chapter 4

1. The first term after the adoption of the Declaration of Independence in which cases were heard was the April 1778 term. In 1778, 15 cases in all were heard; in 1779, 53; and, in 1780, 23. The three-year total was 91 cases, or an average of 30.33 cases per year—well

below the pre-Revolutionary average of 224.40 and the post-1781 average of 279.11 cases per year.

2. See table 1.1.

3. Litigation in the Plymouth County Court of Common Pleas between residents of Plymouth County and residents of other Massachusetts counties rose from 2,330 cases, or 21 percent of all litigation for the period 1725–74, to 2,960 cases, or 24 percent of all litigation for the period 1781–1825. Litigation between residents of Plymouth County and residents of other states rose from 440 cases, or 4 percent of all litigation for the period 1725–74, to 830 cases, or 7 percent of all litigation for the period 1781–1825.

4. See Robert J. Taylor, *Western Massachusetts in the Revolution* (Providence, 1954), 110–18.

5. See chapter 3, note 2, above.

6. Only those litigants who bore the titles esquire or gentleman were so classified. All those litigants were classified as merchants who bore the titles merchant, trader, dealer, or shopkeeper. Those who bore the titles yeoman or husbandman were classified as farmers. Those who bore the titles mariner, seafaringman, fisherman, whalefisherman, codfisherman, boatman, or coaster were classified as seamen. Those who bore the titles drover, truckman, or carter were classified as transportation workers. Only those litigants who bore the title laborer were classified as such.

7. Using the same formula as used in chapter 3, note 12, above, with a 95-percent confidence level and $p = .81$, it was determined that upper-class litigants appeared as plaintiffs against lower-class litigants within a range of 3.2 to 6.1 times more frequently than they appeared as defendants. The number for $p = .81$ was derived from the fact that, based on the 10-percent sample, it appeared that upper-class litigants sued lower-class litigants 1,600 times during the pre-Revolutionary period, or an average of 32.00 times per year, while lower-class litigants sued those in the upper class 380 times, or an average of 7.60 times per year. The number 1,600 is 81 percent of the total of 1,980 cases.

8. Because intratown figures are not derived from a sample, they are not subject to errors of estimation.

9. Plaintiffs from the three upper-class groups brought 505 suits,

or an average of 10.10 cases per year, against fellow townsmen who were lower on the social ladder than themselves, while the four lower-class groups sued those in the upper classes only 146 times, or an average of 2.92 cases per year. For a study that presents data consistent with those in this and the following paragraph, see Thomas C. Haskell, "Litigation and Social Status in Seventeenth Century New Haven," *Journal of Legal Studies*, VII (1978), 219.

10. Using the same formula as used in chapter 3, note 12, above, with a 95-percent confidence level and p = .79, it was determined that the three lowest classes appeared as defendants at the hands of higher-class litigants within a range of 2.4 to 6.7 times more frequently than they appeared as plaintiffs. The number of p, .79, was derived from the fact that, based on the 10-percent sample, it appeared that litigants from the three lowest classes appeared as defendants in suits by upper-class litigants and farmers 860 times, or an average of 17.20 times per year, during the pre-Revolutionary period, while they appeared as plaintiffs only 230 times, or 4.60 times per year. The number 860 is 79 percent of the total of 1,090 cases.

11. Litigants from the three lowest classes appeared as defendants 383 times in intratown litigation, or an average of 7.66 times per year, against fellow townsmen who were higher on the social ladder, while those same lower-class litigants sued those above them only 114 times, or an average of 2.28 times per year.

12. Using the same formula as used in chapter 3, note 12, above, with an 85-percent confidence level and p = .61, it was determined that during the decade 1781–90 litigants from the three upper classes appeared as plaintiffs against defendants from the four lower classes within a range of 1.0 to 2.4 times more frequently than they appeared as defendants. The number for p, .61, was derived from the fact that, based on the 10-percent sample, it appeared that upper-class litigants sued lower-class litigants 280 times, or an average of 28.00 times per year, while lower-class litigants sued those in the upper class 180 times, or an average of 18.00 times per year. The number 280 is 61 percent of the total of 460 cases. Because the range of values, 1.0 to 2.4, never overlaps the corresponding range for the

pre-Revolutionary period given in note 7, above, it can be stated with 85-percent confidence that the three upper classes appeared as plaintiffs against the four lower classes less frequently during the 1780s than they had during the pre-Revolutionary period.

13. Plaintiffs from the three upper classes brought 108 cases, or an average of 10.80 per year, against fellow townsmen who were lower on the social ladder, while litigants in the four lower groups sued those in the three upper groups 78 times, or 7.80 times per year.

14. The 10-percent sample yielded only 16 cases for the decade 1781–90 in which the four upper classes sued the three lower classes and vice versa. When the sample is multiplied by ten, it shows that the upper classes sued the lower classes 110 times, while the lower classes sued the upper classes 50 times; hence, the upper classes were on the plaintiff's side in 69 percent of all cases. Using the same formula as used in chapter 3, note 12, above, with $p = .69$ and with the same .08 margin of error as was identified in the corresponding pre-Revolutionary sample, see note 10, above, it appears that the three lowest classes appeared as defendants at upper-class hands within a range of 1.6 to 3.3 times more frequently than they appeared as plaintiffs. These statements can be made, however, with only a 52-percent level of confidence and hence are not reliable.

15. See generally Bernard Bailyn, *The Ideological Origins of the American Revolution* (Cambridge, Mass., 1967), 301–19; Elisha P. Douglass, *Rebels and Democrats: The Struggle for Equal Political Rights and Majority Rule During the American Revolution* (Chapel Hill, 1955), 10–32, 136–213; William E. Nelson, *Americanization of the Common Law: The Impact of Legal Change on Massachusetts Society, 1760–1830* (Cambridge, Mass., 1975), 101–9.

16. See Oscar Handlin and Mary F. Handlin, *Commonwealth: A Study of the Role of Government in the American Economy, Massachusetts, 1774–1861* (Cambridge, Mass., rev. ed., 1969), 10–12; Richard D. Brown, "The Confiscation and Disposition of Loyalists' Estates in Suffolk County, Massachusetts," *William and Mary Quarterly* (3d ser.), XXI (1964), 534, 547–49.

17. See Nelson, *Americanization of the Common Law*, 70–71.

18. See *ibid.*, 70–71.

19. See Albert B. Hart, *Commonwealth History of Massachusetts* (New York, 1929), III, 526–34.

20. Using the same formula as used in chapter 3, note 12, above, with a 95-percent confidence level and p = .77, it was determined that beginning in 1791 upper-class litigants appeared as plaintiffs against lower-class litigants within a range of 2.6 to 4.6 times more frequently than they appeared as defendants. The number of p, .77, was derived from the fact that, based on the 10-percent sample, it appeared that upper-class litigants sued lower-class ones in 1,810 cases, or an average of 51.71 times per year, while lower-class litigants sued those in the upper class 540 times, or an average of 15.43 times per year. The number 1,810 is 77 percent of the total of 2,350 cases. For comparison of the ranges of error for comparable statistics for the pre-Revolutionary period and for the decade 1781–90, see notes 7 and 12, above.

21. Using the same formula as used in chapter 3, note 12, above, with a 95-percent confidence level and p = .79, it was determined that beginning in 1791 plaintiffs from the four upper classes sued those in the three lowest classes between 2.4 and 6.7 times more frequently than the lowest classes sued those above them. The number for p, .79, was derived from the fact that, based on the 10-percent sample, it appeared that the upper classes were plaintiffs against the lower classes in 710 cases, or an average of 20.29 times per year, and were defendants in 190 cases, or an average of 5.43 times per year. The number 710 is 79 percent of the total of 900 cases. For comparison of the ranges of error for the comparable statistics in the pre-Revolutionary period and the decade 1781–90, see notes 10 and 14, above.

22. Plaintiffs from the three upper classes brought 852 cases against fellow townsmen who were lower on the social ladder than themselves, while litigants from those same lower-class groups sued those higher than themselves only 276 times.

23. Litigants from the three lowest classes appeared as defendants 290 times against fellow townsmen who were higher on the social ladder, while those same lower-class litigants sued upper-class ones only 93 times.

24. See chapter 3, notes 6–21 and 69, above, and accompanying text.

25. Using the same formula as used in chapter 3, note 12, above, with a 95-percent confidence level and with p = .22, the range of the percentage of intracommunity cases is between 10 and 34 percent—a substantial overlap with the pre-Revolutionary Middleboro range of 27 to 47 percent. See chapter 3, note 21, above.

26. Using the same formula as used in chapter 3, note 12, above, with a 95-percent confidence level and with p = .52, the range of the percentage of intracommunity cases is between 36 and 68 percent. Because there is some overlap between this range and the pre-Revolutionary range of 27 to 47 percent, see chapter 3, note 21, above, it cannot be stated with confidence that the percentage of intratown litigation that was of an intracommunity nature was higher after 1798 than before the Revolution. However, because there is no overlap between the ranges for the period 1781–97 and the period 1798–1800, it can be stated with 95-percent confidence that a rise did begin in 1798.

27. Using the same formula as used in chapter 3, note 12, above, with a 95-percent confidence level and with p = .46, the range of the percentage of intracommunity cases is between 39 and 53 percent. For the reasons stated in note 26, above, it cannot be stated with confidence that the percentage of intratown litigation that was of an intracommunity nature was higher after 1800 than before the Revolution, but it can be stated with 95-percent confidence that the rise beginning in 1798 continued after 1800.

28. Using the ranges in note 27, above, it can be estimated that the total number of intracommunity cases in Middleboro for the period 1798–1825 was between 314 and 427, for an average of from 11.21 to 15.25 cases per year. The corresponding range for the pre-Revolutionary period was between 2.38 and 4.12 cases per year. Hence, a significant rise in the total amount of intracommunity litigation undoubtedly began in Middleboro in the late 1790s.

29. Using the same formula as used in chapter 3, note 12, above, with a 95-percent confidence level and with p = .37, the range of the percentage of intracommunity cases is between 23 and 51 percent—

a substantial overlap with the pre-Revolutionary Bridgewater range of 25 to 47 percent. See chapter 3, note 12, above.

30. Using the same formula as used in chapter 3, note 12, above, with a 95-percent confidence level and with p = .36, the range of the percentage of intracommunity cases is between 21 and 51 percent—a substantial overlap with preceding periods. See note 29, above.

31. Using the same formula as used in chapter 3, note 12, above, with a 95-percent confidence level and with p = .60, the range of the percentage of intracommunity cases is between 45 and 75 percent—more than a 30-point variation and a range that overlaps slightly with earlier ones. See notes 29–30, above.

32. Using the same formula as used in chapter 3, note 12, above, with a 95-percent confidence level and with p = .80, the range of the percentage of intracommunity cases is between 68 and 92 percent. This represents a 25-point variation and a range that overlaps slightly with that for the immediately preceding period but not with those for earlier periods. See notes 29–31, above.

33. Out of the 97 suits, 9 involved residents from at least two of the four towns, while 41 from the towns of East Bridgewater, North Bridgewater, and West Bridgewater involved only litigants who resided within the same town. The other 47 cases involved only litigants who all resided within the new town of Bridgewater, which, however, contained two parishes: the old South Parish and part of the Titicut Parish. On the basis of a 45-case sample of cases involving residents of these two parishes between 1780 and 1820, in which 7 cases were interparish and 38 were intraparish, it was possible to estimate that 7 of the post-1822 cases involved litigation between parishes, and the remaining 40 were intraparish. On this basis, it was estimated that 16 out of the 97 cases were intercommunity and that 81 were intracommunity. The accuracy of this estimate was checked by using the following formula from William Cochran, *Sampling Techniques* (New York, 1963), 73–75:

$$d = t\sqrt{\frac{pq}{n}}$$

This formula is a variant of that used in chapter 3, note 12, above.

With a 95-percent confidence level and p = .16 (the proportion of 1780–1820 cases that were intercommunity in nature), the range in the number of intercommunity cases in the new town of Bridgewater after 1822 is from 5 to 10 cases. Hence, the range in the total number of intercommunity cases in the four new towns is from 14 to 19 cases, and the range in the percentage of intracommunity litigation is from 80 to 86 percent.

34. Using the same formula as used in chapter 3, note 12, above, with a 95-percent confidence level and p = .41, the range of the percentage of intracommunity cases in Rochester is between 27 and 55 percent for the 1781–1810 period. For the 1811–25 period, also with a 95-percent confidence level and with p = .49, the range was from 37 to 61 percent. Because of the substantial overlap in these ranges, a mere 8-percentage-point rise in Rochester's intracommunity litigation rate cannot be measured by these samples.

35. This assumption is conservative given the main argument of this chapter: that intracommunity litigation was rising rapidly around the turn of the century. The contrary assumption would overestimate the extent of this rise.

36. Using the same formula as used in chapter 3, note 12, above, with a 95-percent confidence level and p = .46, the range of the percentage of intracommunity cases in Rochester is between 37 and 55 percent for the entire post-Revolutionary period, compared with the pre-Revolutionary Rochester range of 37 to 57 percent. See chapter 3, note 70, above.

37. This assumption is the same as that made with respect to the same towns in the preceding chapter. See chapter 3, text at notes 6–7, 28. Although the assumption will produce some overestimation of the amount of intracommunity litigation in the early nineteenth century, it must be made in order to address the main question in this chapter—which is to compare the rate of post-Revolutionary litigation in each town with its pre-Revolutionary rate. In view of the rising rate of intracommunity as a percentage of intratown litigation in Bridgewater and Middleboro, see text at notes 25–33, above, there is no reason to think that the rate was falling in the seven towns presently under consideration. Accordingly, the present as-

sumption, which holds intracommunity as a percentage of intratown litigation constant, is a conservative one. See note 35, above.

38. The period before the rise for Abington and Duxbury is 1787–1801; the period after the rise is 1802–25.

39. The period before the rise for Bridgewater is 1787–96; the period after the rise is 1811–20. Because the numbers for Bridgewater are estimates, they are accurate at a 95-percent confidence level only within certain ranges. The range for the period 1725–74 is between 2.02 and 3.80 cases per year; for the period 1781–86, from 6.17 to 13.69 cases per year; for the period 1787–96, from 1.81 to 4.39 cases per year; and for the period 1811–20, from 18.77 to 25.39 cases per year. These ranges are derived from material contained in chapter 3, note 12, above, and in notes 30 and 32 of the present chapter, above.

40. The period before the rise for Halifax, Pembroke, and Plympton is 1787–1804; the period after the rise is 1805–25.

41. The period before the rise for Kingston is 1787–1805; the period after the rise is 1806–25.

42. The period before the rise for Middleboro is 1787–96; the period after the rise is 1797–1825. Because the figures for Middleboro are estimates, they are accurate at a 95-percent confidence level only within certain ranges. The range for the period 1725–74 is between 2.38 and 4.12 cases per year; for the period 1781–86, from 1.52 to 5.16 cases per year; for the period 1787–96, from 1.10 to 3.74 cases per year; and for the period 1797–1825, from 10.83 to 14.97 cases per year. These ranges are derived from material contained in chapter 3, note 21, above and in notes 25 and 27 of the present chapter, above.

43. The period before the rise for Rochester is 1787–1802; the period after the rise is 1803–25. Because the numbers for Rochester are estimates, they are accurate at a 95-percent confidence level only within certain ranges. The range for the period 1725–74 is between 3.04 and 4.68 cases per year; for the period 1781–86, from 3.70 to 5.50 cases per year; for the period 1787–1802, from 1.87 to 2.78 cases per year; and for the period 1803–25, from 5.69 to 8.47 cases per year. These ranges are derived from material contained in chapter 3, note 70, above, and in note 36 of the present chapter, above.

44. The period before the rise for Wareham is 1787–96; the period after the rise is 1797–1825.

45. The dates for the litigation rise in each town are the same as in table 4.3 except that the postrise period in Bridgewater is 1811–25.

46. Information on officeholding by Middleboro litigants was obtained from the lists in D. H. Hurd, *History of Plymouth County, Massachusetts* (Philadelphia, 1884), II, 952–58, and from Thomas Weston, *History of the Town of Middleboro, Massachusetts* (Boston, 1906), through use of the index.

47. See Hurd, *History of Plymouth County*, I, 509–10.

48. See *ibid.*, I, 364.

49. See *ibid.*, I, 286–88.

50. See *ibid.*, I, 241.

51. See *ibid.*, II, 1115–16.

52. See *ibid.*, I, 211.

53. *Ibid.*, I, 436–37. See also *ibid.*, I, 390–91; II, 1168.

54. Intracommunity cases are the basis for the averages in Bridgewater, Middleboro, and Rochester, and intratown cases in the other eight towns.

55. Except 1811–20 for the second period for Bridgewater. Because the numbers for Bridgewater are estimates, they are accurate at a 95-percent confidence level only within certain ranges. For the period 1787–96, the ranges are from 1.81 to 4.39 cases per year and from 0.36 to 0.88 cases per year per 1,000 residents. For the period 1811–20, the ranges are from 18.77 to 25.39 cases per year and from 3.31 to 4.48 cases per year per 1,000 residents. See notes 30 and 32, above.

56. Because the numbers for Middleboro are estimates, they are accurate at a 95-percent confidence level only within certain ranges. For the period 1787–96, the ranges are from 1.10 to 3.74 cases per year and from 0.24 to 0.83 cases per year per 1,000 residents. For the period 1811–25, the ranges are from 11.70 to 15.90 cases per year and from 2.50 to 3.39 cases per year per 1,000 residents. See notes 25 and 27, above.

57. Because the numbers for Rochester are estimates, they are accurate at a 95-percent confidence level only within certain ranges. For the period 1787–96, the ranges are from 1.70 to 2.53 cases per

year and from 0.64 to 0.96 cases per year per 1,000 residents. For the period 1811–25, the ranges are from 5.53 to 8.21 cases per year and from 1.82 to 2.71 cases per year per 1,000 residents. See note 36, above.

58. Data for Plymouth are for 1781–96. Total appearances are estimated at 35 percent of all appearances during 1781– 1825, given that 35 percent of all lawsuits for 1781–1825 occurred between 1781–96.

59. There is no inconsistency between the data presented for Plymouth in tables 4.8 and 4.10 and the data presented in the "Increased Citizen Participation in Litigation in Plymouth" section, above. That section makes the point that the number of cases in which only nonlitigious residents appeared tripled after 1797, even though tables 4.8 and 4.10 show that the number of appearances by the nonlitigious rose by less than 25 percent. Any apparent inconsistency arises from the fact that, as litigious residents appeared in court less frequently, suits between them and the nonlitigious also became less frequent. In short, while suits involving only the nonlitigious rose sharply, those in which they were pitted against the litigious declined. As a result, all litigation involving the nonlitigious increased at a slower rate than did Plymouth's population.

60. Data for Plymouth are for 1797–1825.

Chapter 5

1. See table 4.3.
2. See table 4.4.
3. See pp. 99–100.
4. The period before the rise for Middleboro is 1787–96; the period after the rise is 1797–1825. Because the range of error for Middleboro's intracommunity cases per year for the prerise period is between 1.10 and 3.74 and 88.8 percent of those cases are noncommercial, the range for the number of noncommercial intracommunity cases per year is 0.98 to 3.32. Inasmuch as the range of error for the postrise period is from 10.83 to 14.97 intracommunity cases per year and 68.1 percent are noncommercial, the range for the

number of noncommercial intracommunity cases is 7.38 to 10.19.

5. The period before the rise for Bridgewater is 1787–96; the period after the rise is 1811–20. Because the range of error for Bridgewater's intracommunity cases per year for the prerise period is between 1.81 and 4.39 and 84.5 percent of those cases are noncommercial, the range for the number of noncommercial intracommunity cases per year is 1.53 to 3.71. Because the range of error for the postrise period is from 18.77 to 25.39 intracommunity cases per year and 70.6 percent of those cases are noncommercial, the range for the number of noncommercial intracommunity cases is 13.25 to 17.93.

6. The period before the rise for Rochester is 1787–1802; the period after the rise is 1803–25. Because the range of error for Rochester's intracommunity cases per year for the prerise period is between 1.87 and 2.78 cases per year and 73.5 percent of those cases are noncommercial, the range for the number of noncommercial intracommunity cases per year is 1.37 to 2.04. Inasmuch as the range of error for the postrise period is from 5.69 to 8.47 intracommunity cases per year and 59.3 percent of those cases are noncommercial, the range for the number of noncommercial intracommunity cases is from 3.37 to 5.02.

7. The period before the rise for Abington and Duxbury is 1787–1801; the period after the rise is 1802–25.

8. The period before the rise for Halifax, Pembroke, and Plympton is 1787–1804; the period after the rise is 1805–25.

9. The period before the rise for Kingston is 1787–1805; the period after the rise is 1806–25.

10. The period before the rise for Wareham is 1787–96; the period after the rise is 1797–1825.

11. See pp. 100–101.

12. The figures for Middleboro, Bridgewater, and Rochester in this table are estimates that are accurate only within certain ranges. See notes 3–5, above.

13. Hanover never developed a major industry in the nineteenth century as did Abington, to its west. See D. H. Hurd, *History of Plymouth County, Massachusetts* (Philadelphia, 1874), I, 391. As a

result, the town today gives the impression of being a prosperous Boston suburb rather than a decaying mill town.

14. See *ibid.*, I, 317; II, 980–88.

15. Nelson was a member of the Third Baptist Church. See Records of the Third Baptist Church in Middleboro (microfilm in John Hay Library, Brown Univ.). Peirce belonged to the Central Baptist Church, see Hurd, *History of Plymouth County*, II, 988, and Pickens was a member of the Fourth Baptist Church, which was an offshoot of the Second. See *ibid.*, I, 317. For a list of holders of various town offices, see *ibid.*, II, 952–58.

16. Lists of Baptists were compiled on the basis of the records cited in note 15, above, together with the Records of the First Baptist Church in Middleboro (microfilm in John Hay Library, Brown Univ.).

17. See Hurd, *History of Plymouth County*, II, 986.

18. See *ibid.*, II, 988.

19. See *ibid.*, II, 781, 893.

20. See *ibid.*, II, 783.

21. See *ibid.*, II, 577.

22. See *ibid.*, II, 590.

23. See *ibid.*, II, 781, 844.

24. See *ibid.*, II, 591, 783.

25. Quoted in *ibid.*, I, 345.

26. See *ibid.*, I, 345.

27. See *ibid.*, I, 346.

28. Abington Church Records, IV, July 7, 1804 (ms. in Dyer Memorial Library, Abington, Mass.).

29. See *ibid.*, IV, Mar. 17, 1806.

30. See Hurd, *History of Plymouth County*, I, 484.

31. Baptists in Halifax worshipped at the Trunk Meeting House, see Halifax Historical Society, *Map of Old Halifax* (Halifax, Mass., 1975), which was built in 1821. See Guy S. Baker, *History of Halifax, Massachusetts* (Halifax, Mass., 1976), 22.

32. See Hurd, *History of Plymouth County*, I, 454.

33. See *ibid.*, I, 198.

34. See *ibid.*, I, 334.

35. The list of Baptists is compiled from Wing v. Inhabitants of Rochester, Ply. C.P., Aug. 1805, no. 61, in which the names of 37 members of the United Baptist Church resident in Rochester are given.

36. The list of Quakers is compiled from the microfilm collection of Quaker records held by the Rhode Island Historical Society, Providence, R.I., specifically the Birth, Death, and Marriage Records of the Dartmouth Monthly Meeting, 1699–1880 (microfilm reel no. 51), and the Marriage Records of the Sandwich Monthly Meeting, 1762–1841 (microfilm reel no. 44). The records include the names of all adult members of the meeting who attended the ceremonies.

37. See Hurd, *History of Plymouth County*, I, 179–81.

38. See *ibid.*, I, 273.

39. See *ibid.*, II, 1165.

40. See *ibid.*, I, 378.

41. See *ibid.*, II, 1167.

42. See *ibid.*, I, 428–31.

43. Plympton Town Records, II, 117 (ms. in Plympton Town Hall, Plympton, Mass.).

44. See, e.g., Annals of Kingston, quoted in Hurd, *History of Plymouth County*, I, 262; *Records of the Town of Plymouth* (Plymouth, 1892), III, 164, 203, 266; Plympton Town Records, II, 97.

45. See *Records of Plymouth*, III, 315; Plympton Town Records, II, 125.

46. See, e.g., Marshfield Town Records, 1779–1803, at 234 (ms. in Marshfield Town Hall, Marshfield, Mass.); *Records of Plymouth*, III, 349.

47. See, e.g., Bridgewater Town Records, III, 1739–84, at 131, 472–73 (ms. in Bridgewater Town Hall, Bridgewater, Mass.); Middleboro Town Records, 1772–88, at 89, 130 (ms. in Middleboro Town Hall, Middleboro, Mass.); Scituate Town Meeting Minutes, 1743–80, at 65 (ms. in Scituate Town Hall, Scituate, Mass.).

48. See Bridgewater Town Records, III, 1739–84, at 133; Marshfield Town Records, 1700s, at 520; *Records of Plymouth*, III, 164, 203, 226, 266, 293, 296, 298, 315; Plympton Town Records, II, 97, 117, 125.

49. See *Records of Plymouth*, III, 281–82. The town's subsequent refusal to receive a protest signed by several inhabitants in the minority suggests some of the techniques that were used to create apparent unanimity. *Ibid.*

50. Middleboro Town Records, 1772–88, at 75.

51. *Records of Plymouth*, III, 349.

52. Marshfield Town Records, 1779–1803, at 234.

53. See Bridgewater Town Records, III, 1739–84, at 133; Marshfield Town Records, 1779–1803, at 238; Plympton Town Records, II, 129.

54. See, e.g., Bridgewater Town Records, III, 1739–84, at 131, 472–73; Middleboro Town Records, 1772–88, at 130; *Records of Plymouth*, III, 347; Plympton Town Records, II, 134; Scituate Town Meeting Minutes, 1743–80, at 65. But see Middleboro Town Records, 1772–88, at 89, 130; *Records of Plymouth*, III, 394.

55. The courts, as was seen in chapter 3, note 1, above, heard few cases during the war years, and surviving records indicate that town meetings and churches did not pick up any of the slack.

56. See, e.g., Middleboro Town Records, 1772–88, at 276, 360. Towns continued to hear fence cases into the nineteenth century. See, e.g., Abington Town Records, II, unbound page dated Sept. 11, 1816 (ms. in Abington Town Hall, Abington, Mass.); Hanover Town Records, 1727–99, at 349 (ms. in Hanover Town Hall, Hanover, Mass.).

57. See Bridgewater Town Records, IV, 1785–1808, at 47, 57; Scituate Town Meeting Minutes, 1782–96, at 36.

58. See Duxbury Town Records, 1781–1825, at 74 (ms. in Duxbury Town Hall, Duxbury, Mass.); Plympton Town Records, II, 225; Scituate Town Meeting Minutes, 1782–96, at 60.

59. For examples of unanimous or nearly unanimous votes, see Duxbury Town Records, 1781–1825, at 33, 36, 53; Scituate Town Meeting Minutes, 1782–96, at 36. For examples of divided votes, see Plympton Town Records, II, 205, 206, 219.

60. Bridgewater Town Records, IV, 1785–1808, at 84.

61. Carver Town Records, 1790–1850, at 47 (ms. in Carver Town Hall, Carver, Mass.).

62. Scituate Town Meeting Minutes, 1795–1821, at 98.

63. Duxbury Town Records, 1781–1825, at 271–73.

64. *Ibid.*, 329.

65. Hanover Town Records, 1802–57, at May 8, 1814.

66. *Ibid.*, May 2, 1808.

67. These election statistics are derived from the official returns, located in the State Archives, in Boston.

Chapter 6

1. See William E. Nelson, *Americanization of the Common Law: The Impact of Legal Change on Massachusetts Society, 1760–1830* (Cambridge, Mass., 1975), 32–35.

2. See Paul Goodman, *The Democratic-Republicans of Massachusetts* (Cambridge, Mass., 1964), 86–96. See generally James M. Banner, *To the Hartford Convention: The Federalists and the Origins of Party Politics in Massachusetts, 1789–1815* (New York, 1970), 197–215. But see *ibid.*, 210, which states that the dissenter-Republican alliance was "unstable" and "a triumph . . . of expediency over principle."

3. Plympton Town Records, II, 271–72 (ms. in Plympton Town Hall, Plympton, Mass.).

4. *Ibid.*, II, 306.

5. See *ibid.*, II, 315, 396–97.

6. *Ibid.*, II, 399.

7. *Ibid.*, II, 406–7.

8. *Ibid.*, II, 411–12.

9. *Ibid.*, III, 122.

10. *Ibid.*, III, 205–6.

11. *Ibid.*, III, 208.

12. Annals of Kingston, quoted in D. H. Hurd, *History of Plymouth County, Massachusetts* (Philadelphia, 1884), I, 265–67.

13. Carver Town Records, 1790–1850, at 114 (ms. in Carver Town Hall, Carver, Mass.).

14. *Ibid.*, 148–49.

15. *Ibid.*, 155.

16. See *ibid.*, 198.

17. Rochester Town [Precinct] Records, 1770–1869, at 29 (ms. in Rochester Town Hall, Rochester, Mass.).

18. *Ibid.*, 35.

19. *Ibid.*, 36.

20. *Ibid.*, 44.

21. *Ibid.*, 45.

22. See *ibid.*, 49–58.

23. *Ibid.*, 71.

24. *Ibid.*, 82.

25. The author has articulated elsewhere his understanding of the reasons for the rise of party conflict in the 1790s. See William E. Nelson, "The Eighteenth-Century Background of John Marshall's Constitutional Jurisprudence," *Michigan Law Review*, LXXVI (1978), 893, 924–32.

26. See Douglas L. Jones, "Geographic Mobility and Society in Eighteenth-Century Essex County, Massachusetts" (Ph.D. dissertation, Brandeis Univ., 1975), 119–26, 129, 205–6.

27. See James F. Shepherd and Gary M. Walton, *Shipping, Maritime Trade, and the Economic Development of Colonial North America* (Cambridge, 1972), 51–53; Margaret E. Martin, "Merchants and Trade of the Connecticut River Valley, 1750–1820," *Smith College Studies in History*, XXIV, 108–9 (1938–39).

28. See Martin, "Merchants and Trade," 109–10.

29. See *Ibid.*, 111.

30. See William B. Weeden, *Economic and Social History of New England, 1620–1789* (Boston, 1890), II, 614–15, 642–43.

31. See Martin, "Merchants and Trade," 102–4.

32. See Weeden, *Economic and Social History*, II, 608.

33. See Robert E. Peabody, *Merchant Ventures of Old Salem* (Boston, 1912), 9.

34. See Weeden, *Economic and Social History*, II, 615–17.

35. For an earlier dispute over schools, see Marshfield Town Records, 1779–1803, at 253 (ms. in Marshfield Town Hall, Marshfield, Mass.).

36. Plympton Town Records, III, 54.

37. *Ibid.*, III, 60.
38. *Ibid.*, III, 64.
39. *Ibid.*, III, 65.
40. *Ibid.*, III, 85. For another occasion on which a committee report on school-district boundaries was rejected, see Rochester Town Records, VII, 1819–33, at 118.
41. Carver Town Records, 1790–1850, at 252.
42. Rochester Town Records, VII, 1819–33, at 21.
43. *Ibid.*, VII, 119.
44. *Ibid.*, VII, 152.
45. *Ibid.*, VII, 208.
46. Middleboro Town Records, 1802–23, at 288 (ms. in Middleboro Town Hall, Middleboro, Mass.).
47. *Ibid.*, 335.
48. Rochester Town Records, VII, 1819–33, at 142.
49. Plympton Town Records, III, 227.
50. *Ibid.*, III, 229.
51. Bridgewater Town Records, IV, 1785–1808, at 86 (ms. in Bridgewater Town Hall, Bridgewater, Mass.).
52. Duxbury Town Records, 1817–36, at 47 (ms. in Duxbury Town Hall, Duxbury, Mass.).
53. Records of the Second Church in Rochester, Church Book, 84–85 (ms. in possession of First Congregational Church, Mattapoisett, Mass.).
54. *Ibid.*, 86–87.
55. *Ibid.*, 87.
56. *Ibid.*, 88.
57. *Ibid.*, 89.
58. *Ibid.*, 89.
59. Records of the First Congregational Church of Rochester, 1798–1868, II, 30 (ms. in possession of First Congregational Church, Rochester, Mass.).
60. See Middleboro Church Records, 1708–1820, at 58–61, 96 (ms. in possession of First Congregational Church, Middleboro, Mass.).
61. *Ibid.*, 59.

62. See Middleboro Church Records, File Papers, 1826 (ms. in possession of First Congregational Church, Middleboro, Mass.).

63. See *Plymouth Church Records, 1620–1859* (New York, 1920), I, 360–61; II, 560–61.

64. See *ibid.*, I, 380–81; II, 487–89, 518–19, 525–37, 564.

65. See *ibid.*, II, 535.

66. See *ibid.*, II, 515.

67. See *ibid.*, II, 518.

68. See *ibid.*, I, 365–66.

69. See *ibid.*, I, 380.

70. See generally Emil Oberholzer, Jr., *Delinquent Saints: Disciplinary Action in the Early Congregational Churches of Massachusetts* (New York, 1956), 239–41.

71. See generally *ibid.*, 252–62.

72. See Ancient Book of Records of the First Church of Christ in Rochester, I, 167 (ms. in possession of First Congregational Church, Rochester, Mass.).

73. *Ibid.*, I, 165–66.

74. See *ibid.*, I, 171.

75. See *ibid.*, I, 177.

76. Records of the Second Church in Rochester, Church Book, 82.

77. L. Vernon Briggs, *History and Records of the First Congregational Church, Hanover, Mass., 1727–1865* (Boston, Mass., 1895), I, 66–67.

78. Records of the Second Church in Rochester, Church Book, 86. Accord, A Church Book . . . in the Fourth Church of Christ in Bridgewater, 1740–1832, at 98 (microfilm in possession of First Parish Congregational Church, Brockton, Mass.).

79. Records of the Second Church in Rochester, Church Book, 88.

80. Records of the First Congregational Church of Rochester, 1798–1868, II, 31.

81. *Ibid.*, II, 57.

82. Norwell Church Records, Ministry of Samuel Deane, 1810–33, at 98–99 (ms. in possession of First Unitarian Church, Norwell, Mass.).

83. Briggs, *Records of the Congregational Church, Hanover*, I, 64.

84. Middleboro Church Records, 1708–1820, at 93.

85. See *ibid.*, 96–97.

86. Ancient Book of Records of the First Church of Christ in Rochester, I, 169.

87. *Ibid.*, I, 176.

88. See *ibid.*, I, 177.

89. See generally Oberholzer, *Delinquent Saints*, 240–41.

90. See Briggs, *Records of the Congregational Church, Hanover*, I, 62–64, 167.

91. See Abington Church Records, III, Apr. 7, 1785.

92. See Duxbury Church Records, 1729–1825, at 177–78 (ms. in possession of First Unitarian Church, Duxbury, Mass.).

93. See Leonard H. Smith, Jr., *Records of the First Church of Wareham, Mass., 1739–1891*, at 41 (Clearwater, Fla., 1974).

94. See *ibid.*, 43.

95. See A Church Book . . . in the Fourth Church of Christ in Bridgewater, 1740–1832, at April 3, 1806 (Amz. Brett) (microfilm in possession of First Parish Congregational Church, Brockton, Mass.).

96. See *ibid.*, June 6, 1807 (Job Bryant, Levi French, Zebedee Snell), November 15, 1807 (Isaac Curtis).

97. Gay v. Whiting, Norfolk Com. Pl., Dec. 1810.

98. Quoted in Richard E. Ellis, *The Jeffersonian Crisis: Courts and Politics in the Young Republic* (New York, 1971), 190.

99. *Wait* v. *M'Neil*, 7 Mass. 261, 262 (1811) (argument of counsel).

100. For a full discussion of these changes, see Nelson, *Americanization of the Common Law*, 166–69.

A Note on the Sources

Five basic types of source material were used in researching this book: court, town, church, and cemetery records, and local histories.

COURT RECORDS. The principal source of judicial material is *Plymouth Court Records, 1686–1859*, 16 vols., edited by David Thomas Konig (Wilmington, Del., 1978–). The records of the Inferior Court of Common Pleas, the Court of General Sessions of the Peace, and their successor courts are included in this published collection. Also consulted were the manuscript records for Plymouth County of the Superior Court of Judicature and its successor, the Supreme Judicial Court. Records for the years up to 1797 are in the custody of the clerk of the Supreme Judicial Court for Boston, in the courthouse there. After 1797, the records are in the custody of the clerk for the Superior Court at the courthouse in Plymouth. Statistical data are derived from these two collections of court records.

TOWN RECORDS. Every town in Plymouth County has preserved at least some of its records, though few sets are complete for the entire 1725–1825 period. A few towns have published their records, but normally only manuscript records exist and these are usually in the custody of town clerks. Footnote citations indicate the location of town records that were used.

CHURCH RECORDS. Many, although not all, of the local Congregational churches in Plymouth County have preserved at least some records. A handy listing of available records is Harold F. Worthley, *An Inventory of the Records of the Particular (Congregational) Churches of Massachusetts Gathered 1620–1805* (Cambridge, Mass., 1970). This list is not, however, entirely accurate because some of the records referred to have since been lost, and others that could not then be located have been found. In general, anyone seeking information about church records will find it useful to contact ministers, town clerks, and librarians, not only in the particular town for which records are being sought but in neighboring towns as well.

Records of dissenting churches are also available. The Rhode Island Historical Society in Providence possesses on microfilm what appear to be all extant Quaker records from Friends' meetings held in Plymouth County and in the adjacent towns of Dartmouth and Sandwich. Brown University possesses records of Baptist churches in Middleboro, including those of Isaac Backus's congregation.

CEMETERY RECORDS. When lists of people buried in particular cemeteries were in print, those lists were used. Most lists that exist were published in the *Mayflower Descendant: A Quarterly Magazine of Pilgrim Genealogy and History*, 34 vols. (Boston, 1899–1937). However, there were also some separate publications, the most useful of which was William S. Latham, *Epitaphs in Old Bridgewater, Massachusetts* (Bridgewater, Mass., 1882). In the absence of published lists, gravestones were consulted to determine burials in particular cemeteries. In some towns, local cemetery commissions possess burial records, but those records were not consulted.

LOCAL HISTORIES. Nearly every town in eighteenth-century Plymouth County has been the subject of a book-length history. These are of a highly mixed quality, but nearly all of them contain useful information, especially on individuals who lived in the towns. Of greater use than any of the separate town histories is *History of Plymouth County, Massachusetts*, 2 vols., edited by D. H. Hurd (Philadelphia, 1884), which contains articles on each town in the county.

Index